AF433372

Green Thumb Chronicles: The Art of Growing Exceptional Weed

From Seed to Harvest, Mastering the Marijuana Garden

Ryan Miller

© Copyright 2024 - All rights reserved.

The content contained within this book may not be reproduced, duplicated or transmitted without direct written permission from the author or the publisher.

Under no circumstances will any blame or legal responsibility be held against the publisher, or author, for any damages, reparation, or monetary loss due to the information contained within this book, either directly or indirectly.

Legal Notice:

This book is copyright protected. It is only for personal use. You cannot amend, distribute, sell, use, quote or paraphrase any part, or the content within this book, without the consent of the author or publisher.

Disclaimer Notice:

Please note the information contained within this document is for educational and entertainment purposes only. All effort has been executed to present accurate, up to date, reliable, complete information. No warranties of any kind are declared or implied. Readers acknowledge that the author is not engaging in the rendering of legal, financial, medical or professional advice. The content within this book has been derived from various sources. Please consult a licensed professional before attempting any techniques outlined in this book.

By reading this document, the reader agrees that under no circumstances is the author responsible for any losses, direct or indirect, that are incurred as a result of the use of information contained within this document, including, but not limited to, errors, omissions, or inaccuracies.

Table of Contents

INTRODUCTION

Welcome to the captivating world of "Green Thumb Chronicles: The Art of Growing Exceptional Weed - From Seed to Harvest, Mastering the Marijuana Garden." This comprehensive e-book is an invaluable guide for novice and seasoned cultivators, offering a meticulous journey into the intricate craft of cultivating exceptional cannabis.

Embark on a horticultural adventure as the Green Thumb Chronicles takes you through the entire lifecycle of the marijuana plant, from the delicate germination of seeds to the bountiful harvest of top-quality buds. This e-book is a treasure trove of knowledge written by seasoned experts in the field, providing readers with the tools and techniques necessary to cultivate cannabis that goes beyond the ordinary.

The e-book covers a broad spectrum of topics, including selecting premium seeds, the intricacies of soil composition, optimal environmental conditions, and advanced cultivation methodologies. Whether you're a beginner seeking fundamental insights or an experienced cultivator looking to refine your skills, the Green Thumb Chronicles has something for everyone.

In addition to the technical aspects of cultivation, the e-book delves into the artistry behind growing exceptional weed. From the careful nurturing of plants to the nuanced process of harvesting, the authors emphasize the importance of cultivating not just quantity but quality. Explore the nuances of strain selection, the impact of different growing mediums, and the art of fine-tuning nutrient regimens to unleash the full potential of your marijuana garden.

Immerse yourself in cannabis cultivation with "Green Thumb Chronicles," a guide that goes beyond the basics, inviting readers to master the art of growing exceptional weed and unlock the secrets to a truly remarkable marijuana garden. Whether you're cultivating for personal use or considering a venture into the burgeoning cannabis industry, this e-book is your essential companion on the journey to becoming a true green thumb in the world of marijuana cultivation.

CHAPTER I

Understanding Cannabis

The different strains and their characteristics

The vast and diverse world of cannabis cultivation encompasses an extensive array of strains, each distinguished by unique characteristics that cater to a broad spectrum of preferences and needs. Understanding the nuances of these strains is fundamental for cultivators aiming to tailor their marijuana garden to specific outcomes. Sativa, Indica, and hybrid strains are the primary categories, each harboring distinct traits.

Sativa strains are renowned for their energizing and uplifting effects. Originating from equatorial regions, these plants often exhibit tall, slender structures with thin leaves. Sativas are recognized for promoting creativity, focus, and a sense of euphoria. The cerebral high induced by Sativa strains makes them popular choices for daytime use, providing users with energy and mental clarity. Notable examples include the invigorating Sour Diesel, the citrus-infused Jack Herer, and the legendary Durban Poison.

Conversely, Indica strains are characterized by their relaxing and soothing properties. Originating from mountainous regions with cooler climates, Indica plants typically have shorter, bushier structures with broad leaves. The profound, body-centric effects of Indicas make them ideal for relaxation, pain relief, and sleep aid. Cultivators often choose Indica strains for their robust yields and relatively short flowering periods. Classic examples of Indica strains include the deeply calming

Granddaddy Purple, the sleep-inducing Northern Lights, and the physically relaxing OG Kush.

As the name suggests, hybrid strains blend characteristics from both Sativa and Indica plants. This diverse category allows cultivators to experiment with various effects and flavors by combining the best of both worlds. Depending on the predominant genetic influence, Hybrid strains can be categorized as Sativa-dominant, Indica-dominant, or balanced. The versatility of hybrids caters to various consumer preferences, offering a nuanced experience that can be tailored to specific needs. Popular hybrids include the euphoria-inducing Blue Dream, the balanced and calming Girl Scout Cookies, and the uplifting Pineapple Express.

Beyond the Sativa, Indica, and hybrid classifications, the cannabis world boasts an abundance of strains with unique genetic profiles, resulting in a plethora of flavors, aromas, and effects. These strains often arise from careful crossbreeding and selection, yielding a rich tapestry of diversity within the marijuana plant.

Terpenes, aromatic compounds found in cannabis, are pivotal in shaping a strain's sensory profile. These compounds contribute to the distinct smells and flavors of different strains and interact with cannabinoids to influence the overall effects of the plant. Strains with high levels of terpene myrcene, for instance, are known for their relaxing properties, while limonene-rich strains tend to impart a citrusy aroma and uplifting effects.

In addition to terpene content, cannabinoids such as THC (tetrahydrocannabinol) and CBD (cannabidiol) contribute significantly to a strain's characteristics. THC is the primary psychoactive compound responsible for the euphoric "high" associated with cannabis, while CBD offers non-intoxicating therapeutic effects. The ratio of THC to CBD varies among strains, influencing the overall experience for users.

Beyond the botanical aspects, the cultivation environment and techniques employed also contribute to a strain's final characteristics. Factors such as light intensity, temperature, humidity, and nutrient levels all influence the expression of the plant's genetics. Experienced cultivators often fine-tune these variables to optimize the growth and potency of their chosen strains.

In the dynamic landscape of cannabis cultivation, the quest for new and exotic strains continues to drive innovation. Breeders consistently cross different varieties to create hybrids with novel characteristics, resulting in a constant influx of exciting options for cultivators and consumers alike. The exploration of strain genetics, coupled with an understanding of the interplay between terpenes and cannabinoids, empowers cultivators to curate gardens that cater to specific preferences, whether seeking relaxation, stimulation, or a balanced blend of effects.

In conclusion, the world of cannabis strains is a vibrant tapestry of diversity, offering cultivators an extensive palette to craft unique and personalized marijuana gardens. Sativa, Indica, and hybrid strains provide the foundation, each with characteristics catering to a wide range of preferences. Beyond these broad categories, the interplay of terpenes and cannabinoids further refines individual strains' sensory and therapeutic profiles. As cultivators delve into the intricacies of strain genetics and cultivation techniques, they unlock the potential to cultivate exceptional weed with precisely tailored effects and flavors, contributing to the ever-evolving landscape of cannabis cultivation.

Basics of cannabinoids and their effects

The intricate pharmacology of cannabis is intricately woven into the diverse world of cannabinoids, the chemical compounds responsible for the plant's wide-ranging effects. These compounds interact with the human endocannabinoid system, a complex network of receptors and neurotransmitters crucial in regulating various physiological processes. Two primary cannabinoids, tetrahydrocannabinol (THC) and cannabidiol (CBD) have garnered significant attention for their distinct properties and potential therapeutic applications.

THC stands out as the primary psychoactive cannabinoid in cannabis, responsible for the euphoric "high" that users experience. It binds to the CB1 receptors in the central nervous system, particularly in the brain, triggering a cascade of neurochemical events that result in altered perception, mood, and cognition. The psychoactive effects of THC make it a central focus for recreational users seeking the characteristic euphoria associated with cannabis consumption. However, the compound also possesses therapeutic potential, with studies indicating its efficacy in managing pain, nausea, and muscle spasms, making it a subject of interest in medical cannabis research.

In contrast, CBD does not induce the intoxicating effects commonly associated with THC. CBD interacts with CB1 and CB2 receptors throughout the body's endocannabinoid system. Its mechanisms of action are diverse, including modulation of neurotransmitter release, anti-inflammatory effects, and antioxidant properties. CBD has gained widespread attention for its potential therapeutic applications, ranging from anxiety and insomnia treatment to pain management. The non-intoxicating nature of CBD makes it an appealing option for individuals seeking relief without the psychoactive side effects.

Beyond THC and CBD, the cannabis plant contains over a hundred other cannabinoids, each with its unique properties and potential contributions to the overall effects of the plant. Cannabigerol (CBG), for instance, is a non-psychoactive cannabinoid that shows promise in anti-inflammatory and neuroprotective capacities. Cannabinol (CBN), a degradation product of THC, may have sedative effects, potentially aiding in sleep disorders. These lesser-known cannabinoids, along with the more prominent THC and CBD, contribute to the entourage effect. In this phenomenon, the combined action of multiple cannabinoids and terpenes produces a more significant impact than individual components alone.

The entourage effect underscores the importance of the synergistic relationship between cannabinoids and terpenes, aromatic compounds found in cannabis. Terpenes contribute to the distinctive flavors and aromas of different strains and interact with cannabinoids to influence their effects. For example, myrcene, a terpene prevalent in many cannabis strains, may enhance the sedative effects of THC, contributing to a more relaxing experience. Pinene, another common terpene, may counteract some of the memory impairment associated with THC, showcasing the intricate interplay between different compounds within the plant.

As researchers delve deeper into the pharmacology of cannabinoids, the potential therapeutic applications of cannabis continue to expand. The endocannabinoid system's involvement in regulating processes such as mood, appetite, and sleep suggests that cannabinoids could hold promise in treating a variety of conditions, including mood disorders, chronic pain, and neurodegenerative diseases. However, the complex nature of cannabinoid interactions with the human body necessitates further research to understand their mechanisms and potential long-term effects fully.

The legal landscape surrounding cannabis has also played a crucial role in shaping the accessibility and study of cannabinoids. In regions where cannabis remains illegal or restricted, research opportunities are often limited, hindering our comprehensive understanding of the plant's therapeutic potential. As attitudes towards cannabis evolve and more jurisdictions embrace legalization for both medicinal and recreational use, the scientific community gains more significant opportunities to explore the nuances of cannabinoids and their effects on the human body.

While much progress has been made, challenges persist in unlocking the full therapeutic potential of cannabinoids. Standardized dosing, consistent product quality, and rigorous clinical trials are essential components of advancing cannabis as a viable medical option. Additionally, the diversity of individual responses to cannabinoids further complicates the development of universally effective treatments, emphasizing the need for personalized medicine approaches within the realm of cannabis therapeutics.

In conclusion, the basics of cannabinoids and their effects provide a fascinating glimpse into the intricate interplay between cannabis and the human body. THC and CBD, the primary cannabinoids, each offer unique effects and therapeutic potential, influencing mood, cognition, and various physiological processes through their interaction with the endocannabinoid system. The entourage effect, driven by the collaboration of numerous cannabinoids and terpenes, further enriches the complexity of cannabis's effects. As scientific understanding deepens and legal barriers recede, the potential for cannabinoids to offer innovative therapeutic solutions becomes increasingly promising, paving the way for a new era in cannabis research and healthcare.

Importance of choosing the right strain for your goals

Selecting the right cannabis strain is a pivotal decision for cultivators and consumers alike, as it profoundly influences the overall experience and outcomes of marijuana use. The importance of choosing the right strain stems from the inherent diversity within the cannabis plant, with each strain boasting unique combinations of cannabinoids, terpenes, and other compounds. Understanding the distinct characteristics and effects of different strains allows individuals to tailor their cannabis experience to align with specific goals, whether they seek therapeutic relief, creative stimulation, or recreational enjoyment.

Selecting an appropriate strain is paramount in addressing specific health concerns for medicinal users. Indica-dominant strains, with their relaxing and soothing effects, are often favored for managing conditions such as chronic pain, insomnia, and anxiety. These strains can provide a calming influence on the body and mind, offering relief without the intense psychoactive effects of some Sativa strains. On the other hand, Sativa-dominant strains, known for their uplifting and energizing properties, may be more suitable for individuals combating fatigue and depression or seeking relief from conditions requiring a daytime medication option. CBD-rich strains, which exhibit minimal psychoactivity, are gaining popularity for their potential to treat various medical conditions without the intoxicating effects commonly associated with THC.

Recreational users, too, benefit from a thoughtful consideration of strain selection. The dynamic range of effects among Sativa, Indica, and hybrid strains allows individuals to curate experiences that align with their desired moods and activities. Those seeking a social, energetic high may gravitate towards Sativa strains, fostering creativity and conversation. In contrast, individuals looking for a relaxed, laid-back experience may opt for Indica strains, promoting a sense of tranquility and physical comfort. Hybrids provide an opportunity to customize the experience further, offering a balanced blend of effects that cater to diverse preferences.

Beyond the broad categorizations of Sativa, Indica, and hybrid, the specific genetic makeup of individual strains contributes to an even more nuanced cannabis landscape. Strains with distinct terpene profiles can influence the flavor, aroma, and effects of cannabis, adding a layer of complexity to the selection process. For example, strains high in myrcene may exhibit relaxing and soothing properties, contributing to a calming experience, while strains rich in limonene may impart a citrusy aroma and uplifting effects. The terpene and cannabinoid content, combined with the overall genetic makeup of a strain, contribute to what is known as the entourage effect. This synergistic interaction enhances the overall impact of the cannabis experience.

Cultivators, too, play a crucial role in the importance of strain selection. Personal preferences and practical considerations such as climate, growing conditions, and available resources influence the decision to develop a particular strain. Indoor and outdoor cultivation environments each present unique challenges and advantages, impacting the plants' growth patterns, yield, and potency. Furthermore, cultivators may select strains based on their suitability for specific cultivation techniques, such as hydroponics, soil, or organic cultivation.

The economic landscape of the cannabis industry also underscores the significance of choosing the right strain. The market demands diverse products, and cultivators who understand and cater to these preferences can position themselves strategically. Popular strains with well-known characteristics may have higher market demand, but cultivating unique or rare strains can also appeal to niche markets, offering a competitive edge. As the cannabis industry evolves, staying attuned to consumer preferences and market trends becomes integral to success.

The cultural and social dimensions of cannabis use further emphasize the importance of strain selection. Different strains have historically played roles in various cultural practices, rituals, and social gatherings. Sativa strains, for instance, are often associated with creative expression and communal experiences, while Indica strains have been utilized in rituals focused on relaxation and reflection. The choice of strain can contribute to the overall atmosphere and intention behind cannabis consumption, shaping the social dynamics and shared experiences among individuals.

The importance of responsible and informed strain selection must be despite the wealth of options available. With the ever-expanding variety of strains and products in the market, individuals are empowered to make choices that align with their preferences, goals, and lifestyles. Education and awareness regarding the diverse characteristics of cannabis strains enable consumers to navigate the complexities of strain selection confidently. Dispensaries and cultivators, in turn, play a pivotal role in providing accurate information, ensuring that consumers can make informed decisions based on their desired outcomes.

In conclusion, the importance of choosing the right cannabis strain permeates every aspect of the marijuana experience, from cultivation to consumption. Whether driven by medicinal, recreational, economic, or cultural motivations, the selection of an appropriate strain allows individuals to harness the full spectrum of benefits that cannabis has to offer. The dynamic interplay of cannabinoids, terpenes, and genetic factors contributes to the vast array of effects and flavors within the cannabis plant. As the cannabis landscape continues to evolve, a thoughtful and informed approach to strain selection ensures that cultivators and consumers alike can navigate this diverse world with confidence, unlocking the full potential of the cannabis plant for their specific goals and aspirations.

CHAPTER II

Setting Up Your Marijuana Garden

Selecting an appropriate growing space

Choosing an appropriate growing space is a pivotal decision for cultivators, laying the foundation for the success of their cannabis cultivation venture. The environment in which cannabis plants thrive significantly impacts their growth, health, and, ultimately, the quality of the harvested buds. Whether cultivating indoors or outdoors, each growing space presents unique challenges and advantages that necessitate careful consideration.

Indoor cultivation offers cultivators unparalleled control over environmental variables, allowing for precise regulation of light, temperature, humidity, and ventilation. This level of control enables year-round cultivation, independent of external weather conditions. However, the upfront costs of indoor setups, including lighting, ventilation systems, and climate control, can be substantial. Additionally, the ongoing operational expenses, such as electricity for lighting, can contribute to higher production costs than outdoor cultivation. Despite these considerations, indoor cultivation provides security and discretion that may appeal to cultivators in regions with legal restrictions or adverse weather conditions.

On the other hand, outdoor cultivation harnesses the power of natural sunlight, significantly reducing operational costs and environmental impact. Cultivating cannabis outdoors is often more accessible for novice growers, as it eliminates the need for complex indoor setups and sophisticated equipment. However, outdoor cultivation is subject to seasonal variations, climate fluctuations, and potential exposure to pests and diseases. Moreover, the cultivation timeline is constrained by the natural light cycle, limiting the number of harvests per year. Outdoor cultivation is particularly advantageous for regions with favorable climates, where cannabis plants can flourish with minimal intervention.

Greenhouse cultivation offers a middle ground, combining aspects of both indoor and outdoor setups. Greenhouses provide a controlled environment, shielding plants from external elements while harnessing natural sunlight. The ability to regulate temperature and humidity within greenhouses allows for extended growing seasons and multiple harvests annually. However, greenhouse cultivation requires a significant initial investment in infrastructure, and ongoing operational costs may be higher than outdoor cultivation. The choice between indoor, outdoor, or greenhouse cultivation depends on factors such as budget, location, desired harvest frequency, and the level of control a cultivator seeks over the growing environment.

The size of the growing space is another crucial consideration that directly impacts cultivation outcomes. For indoor growers, the available space determines the number of plants that can be cultivated simultaneously. Space limitations may necessitate techniques like sea of green (SOG) or screen of green (SCROG) to maximize yields in a confined area. Outdoor growers can scale up their operations based on available land. However, cultivating too many plants in a limited outdoor space may lead to overcrowding, reducing airflow, and increasing the risk of pest and disease issues. Balancing the available space with the cultivation goals and operational capacity is essential for optimizing plant health and maximizing yields.

Lighting is a critical component in any cultivation setup, and the choice of lighting system depends on the selected growing space. In indoor cultivation, high-intensity discharge (HID) lights, such as metal halide (MH) and high-pressure sodium (HPS) lamps, have traditionally been popular due to their efficacy in promoting robust plant growth. However, light-emitting diode (LED) technology has gained prominence for its energy efficiency, spectrum adjustability, and lower heat output. LED lights offer cultivators greater flexibility in tailoring light spectra to specific growth stages, resulting in improved yields and potency. Outdoor cultivators harness the natural sunlight, and while they don't have control over the light cycle, they must choose optimal planting locations to ensure plants receive adequate sunlight throughout the day.

Temperature and humidity control are crucial factors that directly impact plant health and growth rates. HVAC (heating, ventilation, and air conditioning) systems are employed in indoor cultivation to maintain optimal temperature and humidity levels. Adequate ventilation is essential to prevent the buildup of heat and humidity, reducing the risk of mold and mildew. In outdoor cultivation, selecting a site with good air circulation helps mitigate the impact of high humidity. Greenhouse growers utilize ventilation systems to regulate temperature and moisture while benefiting from natural sunlight. Monitoring and controlling these environmental factors contribute to the overall health and vigor of cannabis plants, influencing their resilience against pests and diseases.

The choice of growing medium is a fundamental decision that affects nutrient availability, water retention, and overall plant health. Soil is a traditional and widely used growing medium, providing a rich ecosystem of beneficial microorganisms. Organic soil mixes enhance the flavor profile of cannabis buds and contribute to the sustainability of cultivation practices. Hydroponic systems, on the other hand, utilize nutrient-rich water solutions, allowing for precise control over nutrient levels. Hydroponic cultivation often results in faster growth rates and increased yields, but it requires more expertise and careful monitoring of nutrient concentrations. Coco coir, a natural fiber derived from coconut husks, is a versatile growing medium that combines soil and hydroponic systems elements, balancing water retention and aeration.

The water source and irrigation system are critical considerations for successful cultivation. Indoor cultivators typically have access to municipal water supplies, allowing consistent and controlled watering schedules. Outdoor growers must consider the availability of water sources on their chosen site and may need to implement irrigation systems such as drip systems or soaker hoses. Efficient water management is essential to prevent overwatering, which leads to root rot or underwatering and negatively impacts plant growth and yields. Collecting and storing rainwater can be a sustainable practice for outdoor cultivators, reducing reliance on external water sources.

The choice of nutrients significantly influences plant development and the overall quality of harvested buds. Cannabis plants require a balance of essential nutrients, including nitrogen, phosphorus, potassium, and micronutrients, throughout their growth cycle. Organic and synthetic nutrient options are available, each with advantages and considerations. Organic nutrients derived from natural sources contribute to soil health and microbial activity, enhancing the overall vitality of the cannabis plant. Synthetic nutrients offer precise control over nutrient concentrations and are often preferred in hydroponic systems. Cultivators must tailor nutrient regimens to the specific needs of their chosen strains and adjust nutrient levels based on growth stages.

Security and discretion are paramount considerations for cultivators, particularly in regions with legal restrictions on cannabis cultivation. Indoor cultivation provides high security and privacy, as the enclosed environment conceals the cultivation operation. Advanced security measures, such as surveillance systems and access control, further safeguard indoor cultivation facilities. Outdoor cultivation, while more exposed, allows cultivators to benefit from the natural environment and sunlight. However, outdoor growers must implement security measures, such as fencing and deterrents, to protect their crops from theft or unauthorized access. Balancing security with the cultivation space's accessibility is crucial for cultivators navigating legal and safety considerations.

Local regulations and legal frameworks play a crucial role in determining the feasibility and constraints of cannabis cultivation. Cultivators must know and comply with local cannabis cultivation laws, including zoning regulations, licensing requirements, and permissible plant counts. Understanding the legal landscape ensures cultivators operate within the confines of the law, avoiding potential legal repercussions. Additionally, compliance with environmental regulations and sustainability practices contributes to responsible cultivation practices, aligning with evolving societal expectations and regulatory standards.

In conclusion, selecting an appropriate growing space is a multifaceted decision that significantly influences the success of cannabis cultivation. Whether choosing indoor, outdoor, or greenhouse cultivation, each option has unique challenges and advantages that must be carefully considered. The size of the growing space, lighting systems, temperature and humidity control, growing medium, water source, and irrigation systems all contribute to the cultivation environment. Cultivators must tailor these factors to align with their medicinal or recreational goals and navigate legal and regulatory considerations to ensure compliance and responsible cultivation practices. The interplay of these variables demands a thoughtful and informed approach, ultimately shaping the trajectory of the cultivation venture and the quality of the harvested cannabis.

Indoor vs. outdoor cultivation considerations

The choice between indoor and outdoor cultivation is a critical decision for cannabis cultivators, each option presenting a unique set of considerations that profoundly impact the cultivation process and outcomes. Indoor cultivation offers cultivators a controlled environment, allowing precise light, temperature, humidity, and ventilation regulation. This level of control enables year- round cultivation, independent of external weather conditions. However, the benefits of indoor cultivation come with significant costs, as the initial investment in equipment, lighting systems, and climate control can be substantial. Ongoing operational expenses, particularly electricity for lighting, contribute to higher production costs than outdoor cultivation. Despite these financial considerations, the indoor environment provides security and discretion, making it an attractive option for cultivators in regions with legal restrictions or adverse weather conditions.

Conversely, outdoor cultivation harnesses the power of natural sunlight, significantly reducing operational costs and environmental impact. Cultivating cannabis outdoors is often more accessible for novice growers, eliminating the need for complex indoor setups and sophisticated equipment. The abundance of natural sunlight and fresh air can contribute to robust plant growth and potentially result in larger yields. However, outdoor cultivation is subject to seasonal variations, climate fluctuations, and potential exposure to pests and diseases. The natural light cycle constrains the cultivation timeline, limiting the number of harvests per year. Furthermore, the location of the outdoor cultivation site is crucial, as factors such as sunlight exposure, soil quality, and access to water sources significantly influence plant health and yield.

Greenhouse cultivation offers a middle ground, combining elements of both indoor and outdoor setups. Greenhouses provide a controlled environment, shielding plants from external elements while harnessing natural sunlight. This allows for extended growing seasons and multiple harvests annually. Greenhouse cultivation requires a significant initial investment in infrastructure, but ongoing operational costs may be lower than indoor cultivation. Ventilation and climate control systems are essential to regulate temperature and humidity within the greenhouse. The choice between indoor, outdoor, or greenhouse cultivation depends on factors such as budget, location, desired harvest frequency, and the level of control a cultivator seeks over the growing environment.

One of the primary considerations in the indoor vs. outdoor cultivation debate is the level of environmental control afforded to the cultivator. Indoor cultivation provides an unparalleled degree of control over environmental variables. Artificial lighting systems, such as high-intensity discharge (HID) lamps or light-emitting diodes (LEDs), allow cultivators to tailor light spectra and intensity to the specific needs of their plants. Temperature and humidity can be meticulously regulated through heating, ventilation, and air conditioning (HVAC) systems, creating optimal conditions for plant growth. This level of control enables cultivators to cultivate strains with specific requirements and achieve consistent results. However, the precision of indoor cultivation demands vigilant monitoring and a keen understanding of the environmental needs of the cannabis plants.

On the other hand, outdoor cultivation relies on the natural environment for light, temperature, and humidity. While this approach eliminates the need for artificial lighting and sophisticated climate control systems, it introduces environmental variability challenges. Seasonal changes, weather fluctuations, and exposure to pests become factors that cultivators must navigate. Successful outdoor cultivation often requires a deep understanding of the local climate, soil composition, and potential threats to the crop. Additionally, cultivators must plan their cultivation cycles around the natural light cycle, limiting the number of harvests per year.

Choosing indoor and outdoor cultivation also affects energy consumption and environmental sustainability. Indoor cultivation, particularly with high-powered lighting systems, demands significant electricity usage. The ecological impact of this energy consumption, coupled with the production of equipment and infrastructure, raises concerns about the sustainability of indoor cultivation practices. In contrast, outdoor cultivation relies on natural sunlight and has a lower carbon footprint. Using renewable energy sources, such as solar panels, can mitigate the environmental impact of indoor cultivation. Greenhouse cultivation, while requiring energy for climate control, strikes a balance by utilizing natural sunlight while providing some environmental control.

The physical space available for cultivation is a critical factor that distinguishes indoor and outdoor setups. Indoor cultivators must optimize the open space, whether a dedicated room, tent, or warehouse. Techniques such as Sea of Green (SOG) or Screen of Green (SCROG) may maximize yields in a confined indoor space. The limited area may require smaller pots or hydroponic systems to accommodate multiple plants. Outdoor cultivators, in contrast, often have more flexibility in terms of space. The cultivation area can be scaled up based on available land, allowing for more extensive plantations and potentially higher yields. However, overcrowding must be avoided to prevent reduced airflow and increased susceptibility to pests and diseases.

The impact of the chosen cultivation space on plant health and vigor is a crucial consideration. Indoor cultivation provides a controlled and sanitized environment that minimizes exposure to pests and diseases. However, the confined space can also create conditions conducive to the rapid spread of issues if not appropriately managed. Outdoor cultivation exposes plants to the natural environment, including insects, wildlife, and soil-borne pathogens. Cultivators must implement proactive measures, such as companion planting or natural predators, to manage potential threats effectively. Greenhouse cultivation strikes a balance by providing a shielded environment while allowing for some exposure to outdoor elements, requiring a strategic approach to pest and disease management.

The cultivation timeline is another consideration that varies between indoor and outdoor setups. Indoor cultivation allows year-round cultivation, with the ability to control the light cycle and environmental conditions. This flexibility enables cultivators to initiate and complete multiple growing cycles annually. The predictable and consistent nature of indoor cultivation contributes to reliable harvest schedules. On the other hand, outdoor cultivation is influenced by the natural light cycle and environmental conditions. The cultivation season is typically limited to the spring, summer, and early fall, with a single harvest per year in many regions. Greenhouse cultivation offers a compromise, extending the growing season and allowing for multiple harvests annually, depending on the greenhouse design and location.

Economic considerations play a significant role in the decision-making process for cultivators. Indoor cultivation demands a substantial initial investment in equipment, lighting systems, and climate control infrastructure. The ongoing operational expenses, particularly electricity, contribute to higher production costs per pound of cannabis. However, the ability to cultivate year-round and the potential for high-quality, consistent yields may offset these expenses. Outdoor cultivation requires fewer infrastructure investments, but the costs associated with land acquisition, soil amendments, and water access must be considered. Greenhouse cultivation represents a middle ground regarding initial investment and operational costs, offering a favorable balance for cultivators seeking a compromise between indoor and outdoor approaches.

The legal and regulatory landscape also influences indoor and outdoor cultivation choices. In regions with legal restrictions on cannabis cultivation, indoor cultivation provides a level of security and discretion that may be advantageous. The controlled environment allows cultivators to operate discreetly, minimizing the risk of legal repercussions. Outdoor cultivation may be subject to more visibility and potential legal scrutiny, especially in areas where cannabis cultivation remains regulated or prohibited. Cultivators must navigate local laws, zoning regulations, and licensing requirements to ensure compliance with legal frameworks.

In conclusion, deciding between indoor and outdoor cultivation is a complex choice that requires careful consideration of various factors. Indoor cultivation offers precise control over environmental variables, allowing for year-round cultivation and consistent results. However, the associated costs and ecological impact raise sustainability concerns. Outdoor cultivation harnesses natural sunlight and has a lower environmental footprint but is subject to seasonal variations and potential exposure to pests and diseases. Greenhouse cultivation provides a middle ground, combining elements of both indoor and outdoor setups. The choice between these approaches depends on factors such as budget, location, desired harvest frequency, and the level of control a cultivator seeks over the growing environment. Ultimately, cultivators must weigh the advantages and challenges of each option to make an informed decision that aligns with their goals and priorities in the dynamic and evolving landscape of cannabis cultivation.

Essential equipment and tools for a successful marijuana garden

Cultivating a successful marijuana garden requires a thoughtful selection of essential equipment and tools, each playing a crucial role in fostering optimal plant growth, health, and a bountiful harvest. One of the fundamental components of an indoor marijuana garden is the lighting system. High-intensity discharge (HID) lamps, such as metal halide (MH) and high-pressure sodium (HPS) bulbs, have long been famous for their efficacy in promoting robust plant growth throughout the vegetative and flowering stages. Alternatively, light-emitting diode (LED) technology has gained prominence for its energy efficiency, customizable light spectra, and lower heat output. The choice of lighting system depends on factors such as budget, space constraints, and the specific needs of the cultivated strains.

Temperature and humidity control are paramount considerations in an indoor marijuana garden, and heating, ventilation, and air conditioning (HVAC) systems are critical in maintaining optimal environmental conditions. Consistent temperature and humidity levels contribute to healthy plant development, mitigate the risk of mold and mildew, and ensure the success of the cultivation cycle. Adequate ventilation prevents heat buildup and optimizes carbon dioxide levels, supporting photosynthesis and plant growth.

A reliable irrigation system is indispensable for delivering water to the plants consistently. While manual watering may suffice for small-scale operations, more extensive gardens benefit from automated irrigation systems such as drip systems or soaker hoses. These systems ensure precise and efficient water distribution, preventing overwatering or underwatering, which can adversely affect plant health. Additionally, cultivators may implement nutrient delivery systems to provide essential minerals and fertilizers directly to the plants, promoting robust growth and flower development.

The choice of growing medium significantly influences nutrient availability, water retention, and overall plant health. Soil, a traditional and widely used medium, contains a rich ecosystem of beneficial microorganisms contributing to plant vitality. Organic soil mixes enhance the flavor profile of cannabis buds and promote sustainable cultivation practices. Hydroponic systems, conversely, deliver nutrient-rich water solutions directly to the plant's roots, allowing for precise control over nutrient concentrations. Coco coir, a natural fiber derived from coconut husks, is a versatile growing medium that combines soil and hydroponic systems elements, balancing water retention and aeration.

Cultivators must monitor and maintain nutrient levels to ensure the optimal development of marijuana plants. Organic and synthetic nutrient options are available, each with advantages and considerations. Organic nutrients from natural sources contribute to soil health and microbial activity, enhancing overall plant vitality. Synthetic nutrients offer precise control over nutrient concentrations and are often preferred in hydroponic systems. Cultivators must tailor nutrient regimens to the specific needs of their chosen strains and adjust nutrient levels based on the plants' growth stages.

The physical space available for cultivation is pivotal in selecting appropriate equipment and tools. For indoor cultivators, the choice of pots or containers and the layout of the growing space directly impact the number of plants that can be cultivated simultaneously. Techniques such as Sea of Green (SOG) or Screen of Green (SCROG) may maximize yields in a confined indoor space. On the other hand, outdoor cultivators can scale up their operations based on available land. However, careful consideration must be given to spacing between plants to avoid overcrowding, which can hinder airflow and increase the risk of pests and diseases.

The choice of lighting, ventilation, and growing medium directly influences the environmental conditions within the cultivation space. Cultivators must closely monitor these variables to ensure optimal plant health and growth. To this end, ecological monitoring tools such as thermometers, hygrometers, and pH meters are indispensable. These tools provide real-time temperature, humidity, and soil pH data, enabling cultivators to make informed adjustments and maintain a stable and conducive growing environment.

Pest and disease management tools are crucial for preserving the health and vigor of a marijuana garden. Insect nets, sticky traps, and beneficial predators can be employed to control and prevent infestations. Regular inspections of plants for signs of pests or diseases allow cultivators to identify issues early and implement effective interventions. Fungicides and pesticides, whether organic or synthetic, must be applied judiciously and by recommended guidelines to minimize the risk of harm to the plants and the final product.

Harvesting and trimming tools are essential for ensuring the quality of the final product. Pruning shears or trimming scissors remove excess foliage during the cultivation cycle, promoting airflow and directing energy toward bud development. When harvest time arrives, sharp, clean trimming scissors are crucial for delicately removing buds from the plant. Additionally, drying racks and containers facilitate the drying and curing process, preserving the harvested buds' flavor, aroma, and potency.

Security measures are vital considerations, particularly for indoor cultivators and those operating in regions with legal restrictions. Surveillance systems, motion sensors, and access control systems contribute to a secure cultivation environment, minimizing the risk of theft or unauthorized access. For outdoor cultivators, fencing and deterrents can protect against potential threats.

In conclusion, the equipment and tools selected for a marijuana garden play a pivotal role in determining the success of the cultivation venture. From lighting systems to environmental monitoring tools, irrigation systems to pest management tools, each component contributes to the overall health, growth, and quality of the cannabis plants. The choice between indoor and outdoor cultivation and the specific needs of the cultivated strains further influences the selection of equipment. Cultivators must approach the cultivation process with a comprehensive understanding of the tools and equipment required for each stage of the marijuana plant's lifecycle, ensuring a successful and rewarding cultivation experience.

CHAPTER III

Choosing the Right Seeds

Exploring seed varieties

Exploring seed varieties is a pivotal step for cannabis cultivators, marking the inception of a journey that will shape the final product's characteristics, flavors, and effects. The vast array of cannabis seeds available in the market presents cultivators with a diverse palette of options, each strain offering unique genetic profiles, cannabinoid ratios, and terpene compositions. Sativa-dominant strains, known for their uplifting and energizing effects, are favored by those seeking daytime stimulation and creative inspiration. These strains often exhibit tall, lanky growth patterns with thin leaves and are associated with flavors and aromas ranging from citrusy and fruity to earthy and spicy. Indica-dominant strains, conversely, are renowned for their relaxing and soothing properties, making them a popular choice for evening use or managing conditions such as insomnia and chronic pain. Indica-dominant plants typically display bushier growth with broader leaves; their flavors may include sweet, skunky, or floral notes.

Hybrid strains, a crossbreeding of Sativa and Indica genetics, offer a spectrum of effects that blend the characteristics of both parent strains. These hybrids can be further categorized as Sativa-dominant, Indica-dominant, or balanced, depending on the emphasis on the genetic traits. Sativa-dominant hybrids may provide a cerebral and uplifting experience with a touch of physical relaxation, while Indica-dominant hybrids offer a more soothing experience with elements of mental euphoria.

Balanced hybrids aim to strike a harmony between the contrasting effects of Sativa and Indica, providing a well-rounded experience that caters to a broad range of preferences.

CBD-rich strains have gained prominence for their therapeutic potential, offering the benefits of cannabidiol (CBD) without the intense psychoactive effects associated with tetrahydrocannabinol (THC). These strains are sought after for their potential in managing conditions such as anxiety, inflammation, and epilepsy. The resurgence of interest in CBD has led to the development of strains with high CBD-to-THC ratios, providing users with the therapeutic benefits of CBD while minimizing the psychoactive impact. The flavors and aromas of CBD-rich strains vary, encompassing earthy, floral, and fruity notes, providing a diverse range of options for those seeking therapeutic relief without a significant psychoactive experience.

Beyond the broad categorizations of Sativa, Indica, hybrid, and CBD-rich strains, the exploration of seed varieties delves into the specific genetic makeup of individual strains. Each strain carries a unique combination of cannabinoids, terpenes, and other compounds, contributing to a distinct profile of effects, flavors, and aromas. Terpenes, the aromatic compounds found in cannabis, are crucial in shaping the sensory experience and therapeutic effects. Strains rich in myrcene, for example, may impart a musky and earthy aroma while contributing to the soothing impacts, making them suitable for relaxation and sleep. On the other hand, strains high in limonene exhibit citrusy aromas and are associated with uplifting and mood-enhancing effects.

Exploring seed varieties extends beyond considering effects and flavors; it encompasses plant morphology, growth patterns, and adaptability to different cultivation environments. Autoflowering strains, for instance, have gained popularity for their ability to transition from the vegetative to the flowering stage based on age rather than changes in light cycles. This characteristic reduces the cultivation time and offers the possibility of multiple harvests per year, making auto-flowering strains an attractive option for cultivators seeking efficiency and faster turnaround.

Landrace strains, native to specific regions and adapted to local climates, provide a glimpse into the historical and geographical origins of cannabis. These strains often exhibit unique characteristics and resilience, allowing cultivators to connect with the plant's diverse heritage. However, cultivating landrace strains may require careful consideration of environmental conditions to recreate the native habitat in which these strains evolved.

The exploration of seed varieties also intersects with the burgeoning field of cannabis breeding, where breeders work to create new and innovative strains by combining desirable traits from different parent plants. This continuous innovation results in a constantly expanding menu of options for cultivators, with each new strain offering a blend of characteristics that cater to evolving preferences and therapeutic needs. Breeders may focus on enhancing specific traits, such as increasing cannabinoid potency, improving disease resistance, or creating unique flavor profiles.

For cultivators, exploring seed varieties involves thoughtful consideration of personal preferences, cultivation goals, and the specific challenges of their environment. Whether cultivating for recreational use, therapeutic purposes, or a combination of both, the diverse world of cannabis seeds provides a rich tapestry of options to suit individual needs. As the cannabis industry continues to evolve and regulations change, the availability of seed varieties and breeding techniques will likely expand, offering cultivators an ever-growing array of choices to explore and experiment with in their quest to cultivate exceptional cannabis plants.

Understanding feminized seeds, auto-flowering seeds, and more

Understanding the diverse world of cannabis seeds is crucial for cultivators looking to tailor their cultivation experience to specific preferences, timelines, and growing conditions. Feminized seeds, popular among growers, are selectively bred to produce only female plants, eliminating the risk of male plants in the garden. Since female plants are the ones that have the resinous flowers sought after for consumption, feminized seeds ensure a higher yield of usable cannabis. This selective breeding process involves inducing a female plant to produce pollen, which is then used to fertilize another female, resulting in seeds with exclusively female genetics. Feminized seeds provide efficiency and consistency in cultivation, allowing growers to maximize their space and resources for the plant's most potent and valuable part.

Auto-flowering seeds represent another innovative category, offering cultivators a unique advantage regarding cultivation timeline and ease. Unlike traditional cannabis plants that rely on changes in light cycles to transition from the vegetative to the flowering stage, auto-flowering seeds automatically begin flowering after a set period, typically two to four weeks. This feature allows cultivators to shorten the overall cultivation time, enabling multiple harvests within a growing season. Auto-flowering plants are often smaller in stature, making them suitable for discreet or limited cultivation spaces. While auto-flowering strains may have slightly reduced yields compared to their non-auto counterparts, the trade-off in speed and convenience makes them an attractive option for cultivators seeking a more flexible and rapid cultivation cycle.

CBD-rich seeds cater to the increasing demand for cannabis varieties with elevated levels of cannabidiol (CBD) and lower levels of tetrahydrocannabinol (THC). CBD is renowned for its therapeutic properties, offering anti-inflammatory, analgesic, and anxiolytic effects without the psychoactive intensity associated with THC. Breeding CBD-rich strains involves selecting plants with high CBD content and minimal THC, resulting in seeds that consistently produce plants with these desired characteristics. Cultivators interested in the therapeutic benefits of cannabis without the traditional "high" often opt for CBD-rich seeds to cultivate plants tailored to their specific health and wellness goals.

Landrace strains, often considered the original cannabis varieties, are native to specific regions around the world. These strains have adapted to the local climate, soil conditions, and other environmental factors over centuries, resulting in unique and region-specific characteristics. Cultivating landrace strains allows cultivators to connect with the historical and geographical origins of cannabis. However, developing landrace strains may pose challenges, requiring specific environmental conditions to thrive. The preservation of landrace strains also plays a crucial role in maintaining the biodiversity of cannabis genetics, preventing the loss of unique and valuable traits.

Beyond these categories, the cannabis seed market continues to evolve with the advent of new breeding techniques and technologies. Regular seeds, representing the traditional and unaltered genetic makeup of the cannabis plant, include both male and female seeds. While they offer natural breeding and genetic diversity, regular seeds require careful monitoring to remove male plants, which can pollinate females, leading to seed production rather than the desired resinous flowers.

In recent years, there has been a surge in the popularity of high-CBD, low-THC seeds, catering to individuals seeking the therapeutic benefits of CBD without the psychoactive effects of THC. These seeds produce plants with a CBD-to-THC ratio that aligns with medicinal and wellness objectives. Breeding such seeds involves meticulous selection and testing to ensure consistent cannabinoid ratios in the resulting plants.

Cannabis breeders have also ventured into creating seeds with specific terpene profiles, focusing on the aromatic compounds that contribute to the distinct flavors and aromas of cannabis strains. Terpene-rich seeds allow cultivators to explore a wide range of sensory experiences, from citrusy and fruity to earthy and spicy, enhancing the overall enjoyment of the cannabis consumption experience.

Technological advancements in breeding have led to the development of stabilized and backcrossed seeds. Stabilized seeds result from multiple generations of selective breeding to lock in desirable traits, creating a more consistent and reliable genetic profile. Backcrossing involves reintroducing the genes of a parent plant back into its offspring, reinforcing specific characteristics while retaining the desired traits. These advanced breeding techniques contribute to the precision and predictability of seed genetics, providing cultivators with seeds that reliably express the desired traits in their plants.

As the cannabis industry grows and regulations evolve, cultivators will likely encounter an expanding array of seed varieties, each offering unique characteristics and advantages. Understanding the distinctions between feminized, auto-flowering, CBD-rich, landrace, and other seed categories empowers cultivators to make informed decisions based on their cultivation goals, preferences, and environmental conditions. The dynamic landscape of cannabis seeds offers an exciting and ever-expanding canvas for cultivators to explore and experiment with, fostering a culture of innovation and diversity within cannabis cultivation.

Sourcing high-quality seeds for optimal results

Sourcing high-quality cannabis seeds is crucial for cultivators aiming to achieve optimal results in their cultivation endeavors. The quality of seeds profoundly influences the entire cultivation process, from germination to harvest, and ultimately shapes the characteristics of the final product. Cultivators should prioritize reputable and reliable seed banks or breeders with a proven track record of delivering consistent and high-quality genetics when seeking seeds. Online reviews, testimonials, and recommendations from other growers can serve as valuable resources in identifying reputable sources. Additionally, choosing seeds from well- established breeders known for their expertise and commitment to genetic stability enhances the likelihood of obtaining seeds that exhibit the desired traits and characteristics.

It is essential to prioritize authenticity and legitimacy when sourcing cannabis seeds. Counterfeit or misrepresented seeds waste valuable time and resources and jeopardize the entire cultivation project. Authentic seeds from reputable sources come with a guarantee of genetic purity, ensuring that the seeds purchased accurately represent the specified strain. Cultivators should exercise caution when considering sources with dubious reputations or unverifiable backgrounds, as these may lead to subpar or unreliable genetics.

Understanding the specific needs and preferences of the chosen strains is crucial when selecting seeds. Different strains have varying requirements regarding nutrients, growing conditions, and environmental factors. By aligning the chosen strains with the cultivator's goals, resources, and experience level, cultivators can optimize their cultivation process and enhance the likelihood of a successful harvest. Thorough research into the characteristics, growth patterns, and potential challenges associated with each strain contributes to a more informed decision when selecting seeds.

When sourcing seeds, cultivators should consider the viability and germination rates of the seeds offered by the chosen seed bank or breeder. High-quality seeds should exhibit a dark and intact outer shell, indicating maturity and potential for successful germination. Reputable seed banks often provide information about their seeds' expected germination rates, offering cultivators transparency and assurance. It is advisable to prioritize seed banks that stand behind their products and may offer replacements or refunds for seeds that do not germinate successfully.

Seeds' storage and handling practices significantly impact their viability and overall quality. Adequately stored seeds maintain their genetic integrity and viability over time, ensuring a higher probability of successful germination. Reputable seed banks and breeders employ professional storage methods, such as vacuum sealing and refrigeration, to preserve the freshness and vitality of their seeds. Cultivators should inquire about the storage practices of the chosen seed source and favor those that prioritize the longevity and quality of their seeds.

Cultivators seeking high-quality seeds should also be aware of the legalities surrounding the acquisition and cultivation of cannabis seeds in their respective regions. The legal status of cannabis varies globally, and some areas may prohibit the purchase, possession, or cultivation of cannabis seeds. Cultivators should familiarize themselves with local laws and regulations to ensure compliance and mitigate any legal risks associated with acquiring and cultivating cannabis seeds.

Cultivating cannabis from seeds offers cultivators the opportunity to explore the vast spectrum of strains, flavors, and effects available in the cannabis world. The quality of the seeds chosen for cultivation is a critical factor that significantly influences the success of the entire process. By prioritizing reputable sources, ensuring the authenticity and viability of the seeds, and aligning the choices with specific strain preferences and cultivation goals, cultivators can set the foundation for a successful and rewarding cultivation journey. The careful selection of high-quality seeds enhances the likelihood of a bountiful harvest and contributes to the cultivation of robust and healthy plants, ultimately elevating the overall quality of the cannabis cultivation experience.

CHAPTER IV

Germination and Seedling Care

Step-by-step guide to germinating cannabis seeds

Germinating cannabis seeds is a crucial and delicate phase in the cultivation process, laying the foundation for a thriving garden. A step-by-step guide to growing cannabis seeds begins with selecting high-quality seeds from a reputable source. Once obtained, cultivators should gather the necessary materials for the germination process, including a plate, paper towels, and distilled water. Distilled water is essential to prevent any impurities or contaminants that may hinder germination.

Cultivators can follow a straightforward and effective method to initiate the germination process. Begin by dampening a couple of paper towels with distilled water, ensuring they are not overly saturated. Place the cannabis seeds evenly on one half of the damp paper towel. Fold the other half of the paper towel over the seeds, creating a sandwich-like structure. Place the paper towel with the seeds on a plate and cover it with an inverted second plate to create a humid and enclosed environment.

Next, find a warm and dark location to store the plates—ideal temperatures for germination range between 70 to 90 degrees Fahrenheit (21 to 32 degrees Celsius). The warmth encourages the activation of enzymes within the seeds, initiating the germination process. The dark environment helps prevent premature exposure to light, as cannabis seeds typically germinate best in darkness.

Cultivators should regularly check the paper towels to ensure they remain damp but not soggy. Maintaining an appropriate level of moisture is critical for successful germination. Mistreating the paper towels with additional distilled water is advisable if they begin to dry out. However, excess moisture should be avoided, as it may lead to mold or fungal issues that can compromise germination.

After approximately 24 to 120 hours, depending on the strain and environmental conditions, cultivators can expect to see the emergence of a small taproot from the seeds. This taproot is a sign of successful germination and indicates that the seeds are ready for the next stage of the cultivation process.

Once the taproot has emerged, carefully transfer the germinated seeds to a growing medium. Many cultivators plant the germinated seeds directly into their final growing containers or pots, avoiding any unnecessary stress or disturbance to the delicate taproot. A small hole can be made in the growing medium, and the germinated seed, with the taproot facing downward, can be gently placed into the hole and covered with a thin layer of soil.

At this point, providing the germinated seeds with the proper environmental conditions for continued growth is crucial. This includes maintaining an optimal temperature, typically between 70 to 85 degrees Fahrenheit (21 to 29 degrees Celsius), and providing a consistent light source. A gentle and evenly distributed light, such as fluorescent or LED grow lights, can be introduced to facilitate the seedlings' transition to the vegetative stage.

Regular watering is essential during the seedling stage, but cultivators should exercise caution to avoid overwatering, which can lead to root issues. Proper ventilation and humidity control also contribute to the healthy development of seedlings. As the seedlings grow, cultivators can gradually adjust environmental conditions to mimic the natural progression of the cannabis lifecycle.

After the seedlings have developed several sets of leaves and are robust enough to handle transplanting, they can be moved into their final growing containers or the chosen cultivation space. Transplanting should be performed carefully to minimize stress on the plants. At this stage, cultivators can also begin introducing nutrient solutions formulated for the vegetative stage to support healthy growth.

As the plants continue to develop, cultivators can observe and adjust environmental conditions, nutrient levels, and other factors based on the specific needs of the chosen strains. The transition to the flowering stage, marked by pre-flowers' appearance, is a critical phase that signals the onset of bud development. During the flowering stage, cultivators should adjust lighting schedules to induce flowering and closely monitor nutrient levels to support robust bud development.

The culmination of the cultivation journey comes with the harvest of mature and resinous cannabis buds. Harvesting should be timed based on the development of trichomes, the tiny resin glands that contain cannabinoids and terpenes. Trichomes transition from clear to milky to amber, indicating the optimal time for harvest based on the desired effects and flavors.

In summary, germinating cannabis seeds is a pivotal step in the cultivation process, and a well-executed approach sets the stage for a successful and rewarding harvest. Each step requires attention and precision, from selecting high-quality seeds to creating an ideal germination environment, monitoring the emergence of the taproot, and carefully transplanting seedlings into their final growing containers. As the seedlings progress through the vegetative and flowering stages, cultivators can fine-tune environmental conditions, introduce nutrients, and

Fertilization is an integral part of nurturing seedlings. While nutrient-rich soil provides a good foundation, supplemental fertilization is often necessary to meet the specific nutritional needs of different plant species. Choosing the right type of fertilizer and applying it in the correct amounts at the appropriate growth stages contribute to the seedlings' overall health and vitality.

Regular monitoring and observation are crucial throughout the seedling stage. Being attentive to signs of stress, nutrient deficiencies, or pest infestations allows gardeners to intervene promptly and address issues before they escalate. Adjusting care practices based on the unique requirements of each plant species contributes to a tailored and practical nurturing approach.

In conclusion, nurturing seedlings for a healthy start involves a holistic approach encompassing soil preparation, watering, light exposure, temperature control, pest and disease management, timely transplanting, and proper fertilization. By understanding and addressing the specific needs of seedlings, gardeners can lay the groundwork for robust and productive plants. Investing time and care in the early stages pays off in the form of thriving and resilient plants that contribute to a bountiful harvest and a successful gardening experience.

Common challenges and troubleshooting tips

Navigating the common challenges in gardening is an inevitable part of cultivating plants, and understanding practical troubleshooting tips is crucial for maintaining a healthy and vibrant garden. One prevalent issue gardeners face is soil-related problems, ranging from nutrient deficiencies to imbalances in pH levels. Regular soil testing is a valuable practice to identify and rectify these issues, allowing for targeted amendments to create an optimal growing environment. Another challenge is pest infestation, where insects and other creatures can wreak havoc on plants. Implementing integrated pest management strategies, such as introducing beneficial insects and using organic pesticides, can help control and mitigate the impact of pests on garden crops.

Water management poses another common challenge in gardening, with overwatering and underwatering presenting potential issues. Inconsistencies in watering practices can lead to root rot, drought stress, and other complications. Gardeners can overcome this challenge by adopting a regular and measured watering routine, factoring in the specific water needs of each plant species. Additionally, environmental factors such as extreme temperatures can contribute to water-related challenges, emphasizing the importance of adaptability in response to changing conditions.

Poor plant growth and development are often linked to inadequate light exposure. Whether gardening indoors or outdoors, ensuring that plants receive the appropriate amount and quality of sunlight is essential. Supplemental lighting can be employed in indoor settings to address insufficient natural light. Conversely, excessive exposure to intense sunlight can lead to issues such as sunburn and heat stress, highlighting the importance of finding a balance that suits the specific requirements of each plant.

Temperature fluctuations and extremes present further challenges for gardeners. Sudden changes in temperature, especially during transitional seasons, can stress plants and hinder their growth. Protective measures such as using row covers and providing shade can help mitigate the impact of temperature-related challenges. Frost poses a significant threat to many plants, and gardeners in colder climates must employ strategies like mulching and covering to safeguard their crops during frost-prone periods.

Soil-borne diseases and fungi contribute to the challenges faced by gardeners, particularly in humid and damp conditions. Root rot, powdery mildew, and damping-off are common issues that can compromise plant health. Employing proper sanitation practices, ensuring adequate air circulation, and using fungicides, when necessary, can help prevent and address these challenges. Crop rotation is another effective strategy to reduce the risk of soil- borne diseases by disrupting the life cycle of pathogens and pests.

Nutrient deficiencies are a widespread concern in gardening, often manifesting as yellowing leaves or stunted growth. Understanding the specific nutrient needs of different plants and providing appropriate fertilization is essential for preventing and addressing deficiencies. Soil amendments and organic fertilizers are valuable tools in ensuring a balanced and nutrient-rich growing medium. However, excessive fertilization can lead to nutrient imbalances, emphasizing the need for moderation and a tailored approach based on plant requirements.

Transplant shock is common when moving seedlings to new locations or containers. Sensitive plants may exhibit stress symptoms, including wilting and leaf drop. Minimizing transplant shock involves careful handling of seedlings, ensuring proper acclimatization, and providing adequate water and nutrients during the transition. Timely and informed transplanting practices contribute to the overall resilience of plants in the face of environmental changes.

Inadequate pollination can pose challenges, particularly for fruiting plants. More pollination can result in better fruit set and yield. Encouraging pollinators such as bees and butterflies, practicing companion planting, and manually assisting with pollination when necessary are effective strategies to address this challenge.

Understanding the specific pollination requirements of different plant species allows gardeners to create a pollinator-friendly environment.

In conclusion, addressing common challenges in gardening requires a proactive and informed approach. Gardeners must monitor their plants, identify signs of stress or issues, and implement targeted troubleshooting strategies. Each challenge can be met with effective solutions from soil-related problems to pests, water management, light exposure, temperature fluctuations, diseases, nutrient deficiencies, transplant shock, and pollination issues. By staying attuned to the needs of their plants and implementing sound horticultural practices, gardeners can overcome these challenges and cultivate a thriving and resilient garden.

CHAPTER V

The Vegetative Stage

Providing the right environment for vegetative growth

Creating an optimal environment for vegetative growth is paramount in nurturing lush and vigorous plants. The development of leaves characterizes this phase of a plant's life cycle, stems, and branches, laying the foundation for robust future growth and ultimately contributing to a bountiful harvest. Light is one of the primary considerations in providing the right environment for vegetative growth. Plants undergo photosynthesis, converting light energy into chemical energy, and a sufficient fair supply is crucial during the vegetative stage. Whether cultivating plants indoors or outdoors, ensuring they receive the appropriate amount and quality of light is essential. For indoor gardening, using artificial lights, such as fluorescent or LED grow lights, can supplement natural sunlight and cater to the specific light requirements of different plant species.

Adequate water supply is another critical factor in promoting vegetative growth. Plants actively transpire and require water for various physiological processes during this stage. However, striking a balance is crucial, as overwatering and underwatering can impede growth. Consistent and measured watering practices, tailored to the specific needs of each plant, contribute to optimal moisture levels in the soil. Additionally, ensuring proper drainage helps prevent soggy conditions that can lead to root rot and other issues detrimental to vegetative growth.

Temperature plays a pivotal role in determining the success of vegetative growth. Different plant species have specific temperature preferences, and maintaining an environment within the ideal range fosters optimal metabolic activity. Most plants generally thrive in temperatures between 60 to 75 degrees Fahrenheit (15 to 24 degrees Celsius) during the vegetative stage. Extreme temperatures, whether excessively high or low, can stress plants and hinder their growth. Adequate ventilation and temperature control measures, such as fans or heaters, create a stable and favorable environment for vegetative development.

Soil quality and fertility are fundamental considerations for promoting robust vegetative growth. A nutrient-rich soil provides the essential elements that plants need for healthy development. Incorporating organic matter, such as compost, enhances soil structure and nutrient content. Regular soil testing allows gardeners to assess nutrient levels and make informed decisions about fertilization. While a well-balanced soil is crucial, attention should also be given to pH levels, as different plants have varying preferences. Adjusting soil pH to suit the plants' specific needs contributes to an environment conducive to vegetative growth.

Appropriate spacing between plants is often overlooked but crucial for optimizing vegetative growth. Overcrowded plants compete for light, water, and nutrients, leading to stunted growth and increased disease susceptibility. Providing adequate spacing allows for proper air circulation and sunlight penetration, fostering healthier plants with ample room for expansive foliage. This consideration is particularly relevant in indoor and outdoor settings to ensure each plant has the space to flourish.

Nutrient management is critical to providing the right environment for vegetative growth. While soil fertility is essential, additional fertilization may be required to meet the specific nutrient demands of plants during this phase. Nitrogen, phosphorus, and potassium are primary macronutrients crucial for vegetative development. Understanding the nutritional needs of different plants and applying fertilizers in the correct proportions contribute to robust and vigorous vegetative growth. However, it is essential to strike a balance, as excessive fertilization can lead to nutrient imbalances and adverse effects on plant health.

Pruning and training plants during the vegetative stage are strategic practices that contribute to an optimal growth environment. Pruning involves the removal of unwanted or excessive growth, redirecting energy toward essential parts of the plant. This shapes the plant and enhances air circulation and light penetration, promoting overall health. Training involves guiding the plant's growth pattern, encouraging lateral branching and a more robust structure. These practices are particularly relevant for crops like tomatoes and peppers, where well-managed vegetative growth sets the stage for abundant fruit production.

Support structures create a conducive environment for vegetative growth, especially for plants with tall or sprawling habits. Staking, trellising, or using cages provides support to prevent plants from bending or breaking under their weight. This is particularly important for crops like tomatoes, peas, and beans, where robust vegetative growth produces heavy fruit. By providing the necessary support, gardeners ensure that plants can focus their energy on growth and development rather than expending it on structural stability.

Pest management is integral to maintaining a favorable environment for vegetative growth. Insects and other pests can pose a threat to the health of plants during the vegetative stage. Integrated pest management strategies, including the use of natural predators, companion planting, and timely application of organic pesticides, help mitigate pest pressures. Regular monitoring for signs of infestation allows for prompt intervention, preventing potential damage and ensuring that plants can thrive in a pest-free environment.

In conclusion, providing the right environment for vegetative growth involves a holistic approach considering light, water, temperature, soil quality, spacing, nutrient management, pruning, training, support structures, and pest control. By addressing these elements thoughtfully and strategically, gardeners can create an environment that fosters robust vegetative development. This, in turn, sets the stage for healthy and productive plants, laying the groundwork for a successful gardening experience and a rewarding harvest.

Nutrient requirements and feeding schedules

Understanding the nutrient requirements and establishing appropriate feeding schedules are critical components of successful plant cultivation, ensuring optimal growth, development, and overall health. Like all living organisms, plants rely on a range of essential nutrients to carry out vital physiological processes during their life cycle. Nitrogen, phosphorus, potassium, calcium, magnesium, sulfur, and various micronutrients are integral to plant nutrition. The specific needs of plants vary across species and stages of growth, underscoring the importance of tailoring nutrient management to meet these diverse requirements.

Nitrogen is a primary macronutrient crucial for promoting vigorous vegetative growth. It plays a vital role in forming proteins, enzymes, and chlorophyll, contributing to the lush green foliage characteristic of healthy plants. Adequate nitrogen is essential during the vegetative stage when plants focus on building robust stems, leaves, and branches. Phosphorus, another important macronutrient, is vital for energy transfer and storage, root development, and flower and fruit production. During the early stages of growth and transitioning to the reproductive phase, plants require higher phosphorus levels to support these critical processes.

Potassium, the third primary macronutrient, is involved in various physiological functions, including enzyme activation, water uptake, and disease resistance. It plays a crucial role in promoting overall plant health and resilience. Calcium and magnesium, while needed in smaller quantities than the primary macronutrients, are equally important. Calcium is integral to cell wall structure and function, contributing to plant strength and disease resistance. Magnesium is a central component of chlorophyll, essential for photosynthesis, and aids in nutrient uptake and enzyme activation.

Sulfur, though required in smaller amounts, is essential for protein synthesis and forming specific amino acids. While these macronutrients include the foundation of a plant's nutritional needs, micronutrients such as iron, manganese, zinc, copper, molybdenum, and boron are equally crucial, albeit in trace amounts. These micronutrients play specific roles in enzyme activation, chlorophyll synthesis, and overall metabolic processes, ensuring a well-rounded nutritional profile for plants.

Feeding schedules are designed to provide a consistent and balanced supply of nutrients throughout different stages of a plant's life cycle. Seedlings and young plants often have specific nutrient requirements that differ from mature plants. A balanced fertilizer with a higher nitrogen ratio during the early stages promotes healthy vegetative growth. As plants transition to the flowering or fruiting stage, adjustments to the nutrient composition become necessary, with an increased focus on phosphorus and potassium to support reproductive development.

Hydroponic and soil-based cultivation methods require different approaches to nutrient delivery. In hydroponic systems, where plants grow in nutrient-rich water solutions, precise control over nutrient concentrations is possible. This allows growers to tailor nutrient formulations to the specific needs of their plants at various growth stages. In soil-based systems, pre-mixed fertilizers or organic amendments are commonly used, gradually releasing nutrients over time. Soil quality and composition influence nutrient availability, and periodic soil testing helps determine the need for additional fertilization.

While establishing a feeding schedule, it is essential to consider the specific requirements of different plant species. Fruits, vegetables, flowers, and ornamental plants may have distinct nutrient needs, and a one-size-fits-all approach may not suffice. Additionally, container-grown plants, whether indoors or on patios, may require more frequent nutrient applications due to limited access to soil nutrients.

Organic and synthetic fertilizers offer distinct advantages, and the choice between them depends on individual preferences, environmental considerations, and specific gardening goals. Organic fertilizers release nutrients slowly as they break down, contributing to soil health and microbial activity. They are generally considered more environmentally friendly and sustainable. Synthetic or chemical fertilizers, on the other hand, provide a quick and precise nutrient boost, allowing growers to address specific deficiencies efficiently. Balancing the benefits of both types can result in a comprehensive and effective nutrient management strategy.

Over-fertilization poses risks to plant health, leading to nutrient imbalances, toxicity, and environmental pollution. Careful consideration of the recommended dosage on fertilizer labels and adherence to feeding schedules helps prevent these issues. Monitoring plant responses, such as leaf discoloration or burning, provides valuable feedback on the appropriateness of the chosen fertilization regimen. Adjustments can then be made based on observed plant reactions and, if necessary, through periodic soil testing.

Environmental factors, such as temperature, humidity, and light intensity, also influence plant nutrient absorption and utilization. In indoor gardening or greenhouse settings, where ecological conditions are more controlled, growers can fine-tune nutrient management to optimize plant performance. Regular observation and plant inspection allows for early detection of nutrient deficiencies or excesses, enabling timely interventions to maintain plant health and productivity.

In conclusion, understanding the nutrient requirements and establishing appropriate feeding schedules are pivotal to successful plant cultivation. A balanced approach that considers the specific needs of different plant species, growth stages, and cultivation methods is essential. Whether using organic or synthetic fertilizers, maintaining a careful balance and preventing over-fertilization are critical to promoting plant health and achieving optimal growth and productivity. Regular monitoring, observation, and adjustments to feeding schedules based on plant responses contribute to a comprehensive and effective nutrient management strategy, ensuring a flourishing and vibrant garden.

Pruning and training techniques to enhance plant structure

Pruning and training techniques are indispensable for gardeners seeking to enhance plant structure, encourage healthy growth, and maximize yields. Pruning, the selective removal of specific plant parts, training, and deliberate manipulation of growth patterns collectively contribute to developing well-structured and aesthetically pleasing plants. These techniques are applied across various plant types, from ornamental shrubs and trees to fruit-bearing crops, allowing gardeners to exert control over form and function.

One primary objective of pruning is to shape plants, removing unwanted or excessive growth to achieve a desired form. This not only enhances the visual appeal of ornamental plants but also contributes to the overall health and vitality of the specimen. Strategic pruning helps create a balanced, open canopy, ensuring adequate air circulation and sunlight penetration. This, in turn, minimizes the risk of diseases by reducing conditions favorable to fungal growth and pest infestations. Proper pruning is essential for optimizing yield by directing energy towards fruit production rather than excessive vegetative growth in fruit-bearing plants, such as apple or peach trees.

Timing plays a crucial role in effective pruning. Winter or early spring pruning is typical for deciduous trees and shrubs, as they are dormant during this period. This allows for clear visibility of the plant's structure and minimizes stress on the plant. For flowering plants, pruning immediately after flowering often proves beneficial, as it allows ample time for new growth to develop before the next flowering season. Conversely, summer pruning can control vigorous growth and shape plants during the growing season. Understanding the specific growth habits and flowering patterns of plants guides gardeners in determining the most appropriate time to prune.

Training techniques complement pruning by guiding the natural growth patterns of plants. This involves manipulating the direction of growth, encouraging lateral branching, and promoting a more compact and manageable structure. Staking, trellising, and using support structures are standard training methods, particularly for tall or sprawling plants. Staking helps prevent plants from bending or breaking under their weight, ensuring a more upright and stable structure. Trellising is often employed in vine crops like tomatoes, cucumbers, and grapes, promoting upward growth and maximizing sunlight exposure for enhanced photosynthesis.

In addition to shaping and supporting, training techniques are crucial for improving fruit quality and facilitating harvesting. Espalier, a method that involves training plants to grow flat against a support structure, is often used for fruit trees. This saves space and exposes a greater surface area of the plant to sunlight, encouraging even ripening and facilitating ease of harvest. Similarly, using pergolas or arbors for climbing plants allows for better air circulation, reducing the risk of diseases and ensuring a healthier plant.

Understanding the physiology of plant growth guides effective pruning and training. Apical dominance, the tendency of a plant to channel energy towards the central or terminal bud, can be strategically managed through pruning to encourage lateral growth. Pinching or removing the terminal bud redirects energy to side shoots, promoting a bushier and more compact plant. This is particularly useful in ornamental plants and herbs where a denser and more aesthetically pleasing form is desired.

To improve yield and fruit quality, fruit trees benefit from specific pruning techniques, such as thinning and heading back. Thinning involves selectively removing certain branches or fruit clusters to ensure adequate spacing and prevent overcrowding. This allows for better air circulation, reduces disease risk, and encourages larger, healthier fruit. On the other hand, heading back entails removing a portion of a branch, typically at the tip. This stimulates the growth of lateral branches and enhances the tree's overall structure, contributing to a more balanced canopy.

While pruning and training techniques are powerful tools for shaping plants, it is essential to approach them with a measured and informed strategy. Over-pruning, or removing too much of the plant at once, can lead to stress, reduced vigor, and delayed flowering. Careful consideration of each plant species' specific needs and growth habits is crucial to determine the extent and type of pruning required. Additionally, tools should be sharp and clean to minimize damage to plants and prevent the spread of diseases.

In conclusion, pruning and training techniques are essential components of horticultural practices, enabling gardeners to exert control over plant structure, form, and function. These techniques serve a dual purpose of enhancing the aesthetic appeal of ornamental plants and optimizing the yield and quality of fruit-bearing crops. Gardeners can achieve a harmonious and well-structured garden by strategically removing unwanted growth, directing energy towards essential parts of the plant, and manipulating growth patterns through training. A thoughtful and informed approach, considering the unique characteristics of each plant species, ensures that pruning and training contribute to the overall health and vitality of the garden, creating a visually pleasing and productive space.

CHAPTER VI

Transition to Flowering

Recognizing the signs of the flowering stage

Recognizing the signs of the flowering stage is a pivotal skill for gardeners, marking a crucial phase in the life cycle of flowering plants. This developmental stage is characterized by the transition from vegetative growth to the production of flowers, a process driven by complex physiological changes within the plant. One of the most evident signs of the onset of flowering is the appearance of flower buds. These small, undeveloped structures emerge at the tips of branches or leaf axils, representing the initiation of the reproductive phase. The buds' size, shape, and color are often species-specific, providing valuable cues about the impending bloom.

As the flowering stage progresses, the buds undergo distinct changes, eventually unfurling into fully developed flowers. This transformation is accompanied by color, size, and fragrance alterations, reflecting each plant species' unique characteristics. The emergence of vibrant petals, reproductive organs such as stamens and pistils, and a well-defined flower structure indicate the plant's transition into full bloom. The timing and duration of flowering vary widely among different plant types, influenced by genetics, environmental conditions, and photoperiod sensitivity.

Observing the plant's overall appearance is another crucial aspect of recognizing the flowering stage. The plant may change stature, with some species exhibiting elongated stems or a shift in growth pattern. Foliage may also change, with leaf size, shape, or color alterations, as the plant reallocates energy towards reproductive processes. Additionally, the overall aesthetic of the plant can be transformed, with the addition of colorful blooms contributing to a visually striking display.

Photoperiod-sensitive plants respond to changes in day length as a trigger for flowering. Short-day plants initiate flowering when daylight shortens, typically in the fall or winter. Conversely, long-day plants bloom when exposed to more extended daylight periods, typically in spring or early summer. Day-neutral plants, as the name suggests, are less influenced by day length and initiate flowering based on other factors. Recognizing these photoperiodic cues is instrumental in anticipating and understanding the flowering stage, aiding gardeners in providing optimal care and support during this critical phase.

Accompanying the visible changes in appearance, hormonal shifts within the plant play a central role in the onset of flowering. The transition from a vegetative state to flowering is regulated by the balance of hormones such as auxins, gibberellins, and cytokinins. As flowering is initiated, there is often a decrease in auxin levels, triggering the development of flower buds. The interplay between these hormones orchestrates the intricate processes that culminate in the formation of flowers.

For many plants, the flowering stage is also associated with a shift in nutrient requirements. As the plant redirects energy towards reproductive processes, there is an increased demand for specific nutrients, with a greater emphasis on phosphorus and potassium. Recognizing these shifts in nutrient needs allows gardeners to adjust fertilization practices accordingly, supporting the plant's flowering and subsequent fruiting phases. Regular soil testing and observation of plant responses contribute to informed decisions regarding nutrient management during the flowering stage.

Environmental conditions profoundly influence the flowering stage, and plants often respond to external cues such as temperature and humidity. Temperature fluctuations, particularly cooler temperatures, can induce flowering in some plant species. Conversely, extreme heat may impact the duration and intensity of flowering. Adequate moisture levels and humidity also play a role, with water stress potentially affecting the plant's ability to initiate and sustain the flowering process. Recognizing the interplay between these environmental factors is essential for optimizing flowering outcomes.

The appearance of pollinators around the plant, such as bees, butterflies, or birds, is a clear sign of the flowering stage. The production of attractive blooms, often accompanied by nectar and fragrance, is a strategy for plants to attract pollinators essential for sexual reproduction. The interaction between plants and pollinators is a vital ecological process, contributing to plant populations' genetic diversity and overall health. Recognizing the presence of pollinators and understanding their role underscores the environmental significance of the flowering stage.

In some cases, plants may exhibit specific behaviors or movements during the flowering stage. For example, certain flowers open and close in response to environmental cues or the time of day. This rhythmic behavior, known as nyctinasty, can be observed in flowers such as morning glories, whose blooms unfurl in the morning and close in the afternoon. Recognizing these distinctive behaviors adds a layer to understanding the flowering stage, showcasing the dynamic nature of plant responses to their surroundings.

Observing the timing and duration of flowering is crucial for planning and managing garden spaces. Gardeners often aim to create a continuous or staggered display of blooms by selecting plant varieties with different flowering times. This strategic approach ensures the garden remains visually appealing throughout the growing season. Recognizing the signs of the flowering stage allows gardeners to plan for complementary combinations of plants, considering factors such as color, height, and blooming periods to achieve a harmonious and vibrant garden design.

In conclusion, recognizing the signs of the flowering stage is a multifaceted skill that involves keen observation of visual cues, understanding hormonal shifts, responding to environmental factors, and appreciating the ecological interactions between plants and pollinators. The onset of flowering represents a pivotal phase in the life cycle of plants, marking the transition from vegetative growth to the reproductive stage. Gardeners with a nuanced understanding of these signs can tailor their care practices, optimize nutrient management, and plan for a visually captivating and ecologically vibrant garden.

Adjusting light cycles for optimal flowering

Adjusting light cycles for optimal flowering is a strategic and nuanced practice employed by gardeners to influence flowering plants' bloom initiation and duration. Light plays a pivotal role in regulating the flowering process, and manipulating the photoperiod, or the duration of light exposure, can be a powerful tool for growers seeking to optimize the flowering stage. Understanding the specific light requirements of different plant species and an awareness of their photoperiodic responses allows gardeners to tailor light cycles to elicit desired flowering outcomes.

Photoperiod-sensitive plants, also known as long-day or short-day plants, respond to changes in day length as a trigger for flowering. Long-day plants typically initiate flowering when exposed to more extended daylight periods, occurring in spring or early summer. Conversely, short-day plants bloom when daylight shortens, typically in the fall or winter. These plants have evolved to synchronize their reproductive processes with seasonal changes in day length, ensuring optimal conditions for pollination, seed development, and overall reproductive success.

For growers cultivating photoperiod-sensitive plants, manipulating light cycles becomes a crucial aspect of cultivation. In indoor gardening settings, where natural light may be limited or inconsistent, artificial lighting systems become essential for controlling the photoperiod. High-intensity discharge (HID) lights, light-emitting diodes (LEDs), and fluorescent lights are common choices for providing supplemental light to extend or shorten the natural day length, influencing the flowering response of plants.

To induce flowering in long-day plants, growers typically extend the light exposure beyond the natural day length during the vegetative stage. This is often achieved by providing artificial light for an additional few hour, effectively simulating longer days. Conversely, for short-day plants, the light exposure is reduced during the flowering stage by interrupting the natural day length with periods of darkness. This manipulation encourages the plants to transition to the reproductive phase and initiate flowering.

Understanding the critical role of uninterrupted darkness, or the dark period, is essential when adjusting light cycles for optimal flowering. Regardless of their photoperiodic response, many flowering plants require a specific duration of darkness to trigger flowering. This period of darkness is integral to the plant's internal biological clock and the production of flowering hormones. Disrupting the dark period, even briefly, can interfere with the flowering process and lead to irregularities in bloom initiation.

A change in the light cycle often marks the transition from the vegetative stage to flowering. For example, a shift from an 18-hour light/6-hour dark cycle to a 12-hour light/12-hour dark cycle is a common practice for inducing flowering in many plants. This adjustment signals the plant that environmental conditions are shifting towards a reproductive phase, prompting the physiological changes necessary for flower bud development.

It is worth noting that some plants are day-neutral, meaning their flowering is less influenced by day length. Day-neutral plants initiate flowering based on other factors such as age, maturity, or environmental cues. Adjusting light cycles may be less critical for inducing flowering for these plants, but optimizing light conditions can still enhance overall plant health and productivity.

In addition to photoperiod-sensitive responses, the spectrum and intensity of light also impact the flowering process. Different plant species have varying preferences for light quality, with red and blue wavelengths playing crucial roles in photosynthesis and photomorphogenesis. Red light is often associated with promoting flowering, while blue light influences vegetative growth. LED lighting systems, with customizable spectrums, allow growers to fine-tune light conditions based on their plants' specific needs during different growth stages.

Controlling the duration of darkness is equally essential during the flowering stage. Extended periods of uninterrupted darkness during the dark cycle are necessary to develop flowers properly. Even brief exposure to light, such as light leaks or ambient light from nearby sources, can disrupt the flowering process. Light-tight growing environments, light-proof curtains, or other light-blocking measures ensure that the dark period remains undisturbed, allowing plants to fully engage in the physiological processes leading to robust flower development.

As technology advances, automated lighting systems equipped with timers and programmable controllers have become increasingly prevalent in indoor gardening. These systems offer precise control over light cycles, allowing growers to automate the transition between vegetative and flowering stages. Timers can be programmed to mimic natural day length variations, providing a seamless and consistent environment for plants to follow their natural growth patterns.

Adapting light cycles for optimal flowering is not limited to indoor gardening; it is also relevant for outdoor cultivation, particularly in regions where day length changes significantly with the seasons. Greenhouse growers may use supplemental lighting to extend day length or provide additional light during periods of reduced natural sunlight. This practice ensures that plants receive consistent light exposure, promoting uniform flowering and enhancing crop yield.

In conclusion, adjusting light cycles for optimal flowering is a sophisticated practice that involves an intricate understanding of plant photoperiod responses, the importance of uninterrupted darkness, and the impact of light spectrum and intensity. This technique empowers growers to manipulate environmental conditions, mimicking natural day-length variations and influencing the transition from vegetative growth to the flowering stage. Whether cultivating photoperiod-sensitive or day-neutral plants, precise control over light cycles is a valuable tool for gardeners seeking to maximize the flowering potential of their plants and achieve optimal yields. Advances in lighting technology and automation further facilitate this practice, providing growers with the means to create tailored environments that support the natural growth patterns of their plants.

Managing nutrient needs during the transition

Managing nutrient needs during the transition from one growth stage to another is critical to successful plant cultivation, ensuring a seamless shift in physiological processes and sustained health. The transition phase, often marked by changes such as the onset of flowering or the switch from vegetative to reproductive growth, demands careful attention to nutrient management to support the plant's evolving requirements. As plants undergo these shifts, there are dynamic changes in their metabolic activities, nutrient uptake, and resource allocation. Successful nutrient management during the transition phase involves a nuanced understanding of plants' specific needs during this period, informed by factors such as genetics, environmental conditions, and the plant's overall health.

One of the key considerations in managing nutrient needs during the transition is recognizing the changing demand for certain essential elements. As plants transition from vegetative growth to flowering, there is often a shift in the emphasis on different nutrients. While nitrogen (N) is crucial for lush, vegetative growth, it becomes less of a priority during flowering. Phosphorus (P) and potassium (K), on the other hand, take center stage as they play pivotal roles in flower and fruit development. Phosphorus is essential for energy transfer and root development, while potassium contributes to plant health, stress tolerance, and flower quality. Adjusting nutrient formulations to reflect these changing demands ensures that plants receive the necessary elements to support their transition and subsequent reproductive phases.

Regular monitoring of nutrient levels in the growing medium or soil is indispensable during the transition phase. Soil testing provides valuable insights into the nutrient status, allowing growers to identify deficiencies or excesses that may impact plant health and performance. Understanding the baseline nutrient levels and the plant's requirements enables growers to make informed decisions about adjusting fertilization practices. Soil amendments or targeted fertilization may be necessary to address specific nutrient imbalances and create an optimal environment for the transitioning plants.

In addition to adjusting nutrient formulations, the nutrient delivery method also merits consideration during the transition phase. For plants grown in soil, the choice of organic amendments or synthetic fertilizers and application rates becomes crucial. Organic matter contributes to soil structure, microbial activity, and nutrient retention, benefiting plant health. On the other hand, synthetic fertilizers offer precise control over nutrient concentrations, allowing growers to tailor formulations to meet the specific needs of transitioning plants. In hydroponic or soilless growing systems, nutrient solutions can be adjusted to accommodate changing requirements, providing a dynamic and controlled environment for plant development. Maintaining proper pH levels in the growing medium is another essential aspect of nutrient management during the transition. Changes in pH can influence nutrient availability and uptake by plants. For example, phosphorus becomes less available in alkaline soils, emphasizing the importance of maintaining an appropriate pH range to ensure optimal nutrient absorption. Regular pH monitoring and adjustments contribute to a stable and conducive growing environment, minimizing potential nutrient-related challenges during the transition phase.

The timing of nutrient applications is critical during the transition, aligning with the plant's shifting metabolic priorities. Preparing plants for the transition by gradually adjusting nutrient levels in the lead-up to flowering or other significant changes helps minimize stress. It supports a smooth shift in growth stages. This strategic approach involves providing a nutrient-rich environment during the latter part of the vegetative phase, preparing plants for the increased demands of the upcoming reproductive phase. Timely nutrient applications during the transition contribute to overall plant resilience, health, and the successful initiation of flowering or other reproductive processes.

Environmental conditions such as temperature, humidity, and light intensity influence nutrient uptake and utilization during the transition phase. Changes in these factors can impact the rate of plant metabolism and nutrient requirements. For example, increased light intensity during flowering may enhance photosynthesis, leading to higher nutrient demands. Similarly, temperature fluctuations can influence nutrient absorption rates and transpiration. Adjusting nutrient management practices to accommodate these environmental variables ensures that plants receive optimal nutrition tailored to the prevailing growing conditions.

In hydroponic or controlled indoor environments, where environmental conditions are meticulously managed, nutrient delivery systems can be fine-tuned to address the changing needs of transitioning plants. Automated systems with programmable controllers allow precise control over nutrient concentrations, ensuring that plants receive a customized nutrient blend throughout the transition phase. This level of control is precious in indoor gardening, where external factors are closely regulated to create an optimal growing environment.

Managing nutrient needs during the transition phase extends beyond macronutrients like nitrogen, phosphorus, and potassium, including micronutrients.

These trace elements, including iron, manganese, zinc, copper, molybdenum, and boron, play essential roles in various physiological processes, especially during periods of heightened metabolic activity such as flowering. Monitoring and addressing micronutrient deficiencies or imbalances are crucial for preventing stress-related issues and supporting transitioning plants' overall health and vigor.

The overall health and resilience of plants during the transition phase are influenced by nutrient availability and beneficial microorganisms in the soil or growing medium. Mycorrhizal fungi, for example, form symbiotic relationships with plant roots, enhancing nutrient uptake and improving plant resistance to stress. Incorporating organic matter, compost, or microbial inoculants into the growing medium fosters a healthy soil microbiome, contributing to nutrient cycling and overall plant well-being. These holistic approaches to nutrient management support the transition process and set the stage for robust flowering and reproductive success.

In conclusion, managing nutrient needs during the transition phase is a dynamic and multifaceted practice involving a nuanced understanding of changing plant requirements, carefully monitoring nutrient levels and strategic adjustments to fertilization practices. Whether growing in soil, hydroponic systems, or other controlled environments, growers must tailor their nutrient management strategies to meet the specific demands of transitioning plants. By recognizing the shifting emphasis on different nutrients, optimizing nutrient delivery systems, adjusting pH levels, considering environmental variables, and addressing micronutrient requirements, gardeners can ensure that plants transition smoothly, setting the stage for robust flowering, fruiting, and overall reproductive success.

CHAPTER VII

Flowering Stage: Care and Techniques

Monitoring and supporting bud development

The pivotal stage of monitoring and supporting bud development is a crucial chapter in the journey of cannabis cultivation, where cultivators witness the culmination of their efforts in the form of resinous and potent buds. As the plants transition from the vegetative to the flowering stage, meticulous attention to detail becomes paramount. The chapter delves into the intricate dance between environmental factors, nutrient management, and the plant's internal processes, all working to facilitate robust bud development.

Monitoring bud development begins with a keen observation of the flowering phase initiation. Cultivators eagerly anticipate pre-flowers appearance, indicative of the plant's shift into the reproductive stage. Timing is of the essence during this phase, as it marks the optimal moment to adjust environmental conditions and nutrient ratios to accommodate the specific needs of flowering plants. The chapter emphasizes the importance of a seamless transition, ensuring that the plants receive the right signals to initiate bud formation without unnecessary stress.

Environmental factors play a pivotal role in supporting healthy bud development. Light cycles, in particular, come under scrutiny as cultivators adjust the duration of light exposure to simulate the natural changes in day length that trigger flowering in cannabis plants. The careful management of light intensity, spectrum, and duration ensures that the plants receive the right signals for prolific bud development. The chapter guides cultivators through the nuances of adjusting light cycles, striking a delicate balance to encourage flowering while preventing light-related stress that could compromise bud quality.

Temperature and humidity control emerge as critical elements during bud development. The chapter details the optimal temperature ranges for flowering cannabis plants, avoiding extremes that could impede bud growth or lead to undesirable outcomes such as hermaphroditism. Likewise, maintaining an appropriate humidity level becomes paramount to prevent issues like mold or mildew, safeguarding the delicate buds as they progress through their growth phases. Cultivators learn to fine-tune their environmental controls, creating an ideal setting for robust bud formation.

Nutrient management takes center stage in supporting bud development, with the chapter emphasizing the shift in nutrient requirements during the flowering stage. Cultivators navigate the intricate dance of providing essential macronutrients and micronutrients tailored to the specific needs of flowering plants. The careful calibration of nutrient ratios and awareness of potential deficiencies or excesses ensure that the plants receive the nourishment necessary for vigorous bud development. The chapter guides cultivators through crafting a nutrient schedule that aligns with the dynamic demands of the flowering phase.

As the buds mature, the importance of supporting their development through strategic pruning and training techniques becomes evident. The chapter explores methods such as topping, low-stress training (LST), and defoliation to optimize light penetration and airflow, encouraging even bud development across the plant canopy. These techniques enhance bud size and density and mitigate the risk of mold or pest issues by promoting a healthy microclimate around the developing buds. The chapter provides a comprehensive guide to the nuanced art of pruning and training, empowering cultivators to shape their plants for maximum bud potential.

In addition to environmental and nutritional considerations, cultivators delve into understanding the plant's natural lifecycle and the progression of bud development stages. The chapter unfolds the intricacies of bud formation, from the emergence of small, delicate structures known as calyxes to the gradual clustering and maturation of resin glands. Cultivators gain insights into recognizing the signs of a healthy bud development trajectory, enabling them to intervene promptly if issues arise. The chapter acts as a mentor, guiding cultivators through the visual cues and timelines associated with each stage of bud development.

The role of genetics in influencing bud development takes center stage, with the chapter shedding light on the importance of selecting high-quality cannabis strains known for their desirable bud characteristics. Cultivators learn to appreciate the unique traits and growth patterns of different strains, allowing them to tailor their cultivation techniques to maximize the genetic potential of each plant. The chapter emphasizes the significance of sourcing reliable genetics and its role in achieving consistently impressive bud yields.

As buds progress, the chapter addresses the significance of monitoring trichome development, those resinous structures that house the plant's cannabinoids and terpenes. Cultivators learn to decipher the changes in trichome color, transitioning from clear to milky to amber, as a critical indicator of the optimal harvest window. Understanding trichome development becomes a skill cultivators hone, enabling them to harvest at the peak of cannabinoid and terpene production for the most potent and flavorful buds.

The section on monitoring and supporting bud development transcends the technical aspects, delving into the artistry and intuition that seasoned cultivators bring to their craft. It encourages cultivators to forge a connection with their plants, attuning themselves to the subtle signals and rhythms of the flowering phase. By understanding the plant's responses and adapting cultivation practices accordingly, cultivators elevate their ability to nurture healthy, resin-rich buds that testify to their expertise and dedication.

In conclusion, the chapter on monitoring and supporting bud development serves as a comprehensive guide for cultivators navigating the intricate landscape of the flowering stage. From environmental controls to nutrient management, genetic considerations, and the nuanced art of pruning, the chapter provides a holistic approach to ensuring robust bud development. Cultivators embark on a journey of heightened awareness, where the harmonious interplay of factors converges to yield exceptional buds. Through this section, cultivators gain practical knowledge and cultivate a deeper appreciation for the dynamic and rewarding process of shepherding cannabis plants through their flowering phase, ultimately yielding bountiful and high-quality buds.

Controlling pests and diseases during flowering

Controlling pests and diseases during the flowering stage is a critical aspect of plant management that requires a strategic and vigilant approach. The transition to flowering represents a crucial phase in the life cycle of plants, where they allocate significant resources to reproductive processes. During this period, plants may become more vulnerable to various pests and diseases, making it imperative for growers to implement effective control measures. Pests, ranging from insects to mites and diseases caused by fungi, bacteria, or viruses, pose potential threats to flowering plants' overall health and yield. Successful pest and disease control during flowering involves a combination of preventative practices, early detection, and targeted interventions to mitigate risks and safeguard the plant's reproductive success.

Preventative practices form the foundation of pest and disease control strategies during the flowering stage. Creating a healthy and resilient growing environment is essential in minimizing the susceptibility of plants to potential threats. This includes maintaining proper plant spacing to ensure adequate air circulation, which reduces the risk of fungal diseases. Implementing good hygiene practices, such as removing debris and fallen leaves, helps eliminate potential breeding grounds for pests and pathogens. Additionally, selecting disease-resistant varieties and practicing crop rotation can contribute to a more robust defense against common pests and diseases.

Regular monitoring of plants during the flowering stage is crucial for early detection of any signs of pest infestations or diseases. Visual inspection of leaves, flowers, and stems allows growers to identify abnormalities such as discoloration, wilting, or unusual growth patterns. The use of magnifying tools may aid in spotting tiny pests like spider mites or aphids that may go unnoticed by the naked eye. Early detection allows growers to intervene promptly, minimizing the potential damage caused by pests or diseases.

Integrated pest management (IPM) is a comprehensive approach that combines various strategies to control pests and diseases in an environmentally responsible manner. IPM during the flowering stage involves carefully integrating cultural, mechanical, biological, and chemical control methods. Cultural practices, such as proper sanitation and planting resistant varieties, create an inhospitable environment for pests and diseases.

Mechanical controls include physically removing pests or using barriers to prevent their access. Biological controls involve the introduction of natural predators or beneficial organisms that feed on pests, helping to maintain a balanced ecosystem. Chemical controls, such as insecticides or fungicides, are employed judiciously and by recommended guidelines to target specific pests or diseases.

Companion planting is a valuable strategy for controlling pests during flowering, leveraging the natural properties of certain plants to repel or deter harmful insects. Planting companion crops that emit insect-repelling compounds can act as a protective barrier for flowering plants. For example, aromatic herbs like basil or marigolds are known to repel pests and may be strategically planted alongside blooming crops to enhance pest resistance. Companion planting contributes to pest control and supports a biodiverse and resilient garden ecosystem.

Insect pests during flowering can include a variety of species, ranging from aphids and thrips to caterpillars and beetles. Aphids, for instance, feed on plant sap and can transmit viruses, while thrips cause damage by puncturing plant cells and feeding on the released sap. Caterpillars and beetles may chew on leaves and flowers, leading to aesthetic damage and potentially impacting reproductive structures. Employing physical barriers such as row covers or deploying sticky traps can help prevent entry or capture pests, especially in outdoor settings.

Biological control methods, such as introducing beneficial insects or predatory mites, are crucial in managing pests without chemical interventions during flowering. Ladybugs, lacewings, and predatory beetles are beneficial insects that feed on aphids, mites, and other harmful pests. These natural predators contribute to a balanced ecosystem, keeping pest populations in check. In greenhouse or indoor growing environments, releasing beneficial organisms strategically can provide effective pest control without disrupting the flowering stage.

Fungal diseases are common concerns during flowering, as the conditions favoring flowering can also create a conducive environment for fungal growth. Powdery mildew, downy mildew, and botrytis are fungal diseases affecting flowering plants. Powdery mildew manifests as white, fine spots on leaves, while downy mildew appears as yellow or brown patches on the undersides of leaves. Botrytis, or gray mold, thrives in high humidity conditions and can cause flower buds to rot. Preventative measures such as proper spacing, adequate ventilation, and avoiding overhead watering can help reduce the risk of fungal diseases.

When used as part of an integrated approach, Fungicides can effectively control fungal diseases during flowering. Selecting fungicides with low toxicity and following recommended application rates are crucial to minimize any potential negative impact on plant health. Copper-based fungicides, neem oil, and biological fungicides containing beneficial microorganisms can be employed to combat fungal diseases. Additionally, applying fungicides preventatively, especially in conditions conducive to fungal growth, can be an effective strategy to protect flowering plants.

Though less common than fungal diseases, viral diseases can also pose threats during flowering. Aphids and other sap-sucking insects can transmit viruses from infected plants to healthy ones. Once a plant is infected with a virus, there is often limited direct control, and efforts may focus on preventing the spread of the disease. Managing aphid populations through insecticidal soaps, neem oil, or biological controls can reduce the risk of viral transmission. Removing and isolating infected plants is essential to prevent the spread of viruses to healthy plants in the vicinity.

Environmental factors play a significant role in influencing the prevalence of pests and diseases during flowering. Maintaining optimal growing conditions, including proper humidity levels, adequate air circulation, and appropriate watering practices, contributes to plant resilience. Excessive moisture, for example, can create conditions favorable for fungal diseases, while water stress may make plants more susceptible to pest infestations. Monitoring and adjusting environmental conditions as needed help create an unfavorable environment for pests and diseases, promoting overall plant health.

In conclusion, controlling pests and diseases during flowering is a multifaceted task that demands a proactive and integrated approach. Preventative measures, early detection, and combining cultural, mechanical, biological, and chemical control methods contribute to effective pest and disease management. The careful selection of control strategies, focusing on minimizing environmental impact, ensures that flowering plants remain healthy and productive. By implementing these practices, growers can navigate the challenges posed by pests and diseases, safeguarding the integrity of the flowering stage and ensuring the successful development of fruits and seeds.

Maximizing resin production for potent buds

Maximizing resin production for potent buds is a crucial goal for cannabis cultivators seeking to enhance the potency and overall quality of their harvest. Resin, the sticky, trichome-rich substance the plant produces, contains cannabinoids, terpenes, and other compounds responsible for the plant's therapeutic and psychoactive effects. Achieving high resin production is particularly crucial for those cultivating cannabis for medicinal or recreational use, as it directly correlates with the potency and efficacy of the final product. To maximize resin production, growers employ a combination of genetic selection, environmental optimization, and targeted cultivation practices.

Genetic selection plays a foundational role in determining the resin-producing potential of cannabis plants. Choosing strains known for high resin production, potent cannabinoid profiles, and desirable terpene profiles sets the stage for a successful harvest. Indica and hybrid strains, renowned for their resinous buds and robust cannabinoid content, are often favored by growers aiming for potent end products. Additionally, selecting phenotypes within a given strain that exhibit enhanced resin production during the flowering stage contributes to maximizing the desired traits.

Creating an optimal growing environment is paramount for maximizing resin production. Environmental factors such as light intensity, spectrum, temperature, humidity, and airflow significantly influence trichome development and resin production. Providing plants with the right spectrum and intensity of light during the flowering stage is crucial, as trichomes are the plant's response to environmental stressors, primarily ultraviolet (UV) light. High-pressure sodium (HPS) and light-emitting diode (LED) grow lights tailored to the flowering spectrum can stimulate trichome production and enhance resin content.

Controlling temperature and humidity levels is equally critical for resin production. A slightly cooler temperature during the flowering stage, 65 to 80 degrees Fahrenheit (18 to 27 degrees Celsius), can stimulate trichome development without compromising plant health. Maintaining optimal humidity levels, typically lower during the flowering stage to minimize the risk of mold or mildew, also contributes to resin quality. Adequate airflow helps prevent stagnant air around the plant, reducing the risk of pests and diseases while promoting trichome development.

Nutrient management plays a pivotal role in maximizing resin production. Adjusting the nutrient regimen to emphasize phosphorus and potassium while moderating nitrogen during the flowering stage supports robust trichome development and resin synthesis. Phosphorus, in particular, is crucial for energy transfer and contributes to the plant's ability to produce adenosine triphosphate (ATP), a key component in resin formation. Potassium enhances overall plant health and stress tolerance and contributes to resin quality. Balancing nutrient levels and avoiding excesses or deficiencies ensure the plant has the resources to produce ample resin.

Strategic pruning and training techniques are employed to maximize resin production by optimizing light penetration and air circulation. Removing unnecessary foliage, notably lower fan leaves that receive less light redirects the plant's energy toward bud development and resin production in the canopy. Techniques such as lollipopping, defoliation, and super cropping help create an open canopy, allowing light to reach lower bud sites and encouraging trichome development throughout the plant. These practices also contribute to better air circulation, reducing the risk of moisture-related issues.

Timing is a crucial factor in maximizing resin production. Understanding the plant's life cycle and identifying the optimal harvest window is essential for preserving the highest levels of cannabinoids and terpenes. Harvesting too early or too late can produce suboptimal resin content and potency. Monitoring trichome development using a magnifying tool and observing the shift from clear to cloudy or amber trichomes signals the ideal time for harvest. Harvesting during the peak resin production phase ensures the highest concentration of cannabinoids and terpenes.

When applied judiciously, environmental stressors can trigger a defensive response in plants, leading to increased resin production. Techniques such as manipulating light cycles, subjecting plants to controlled temperature fluctuations, or inducing water stress (held dehydration) during the final days before harvest can stimulate trichome development. These stress-induced responses are the plant's adaptive mechanisms to protect itself from potential threats, and when harnessed strategically, they contribute to enhanced resin production.

Advanced cultivation techniques, such as hydroponics or aeroponics, give growers precise control over nutrient delivery and environmental conditions, offering opportunities to maximize resin production. These soilless systems enable growers to fine-tune nutrient concentrations, pH levels, and other parameters, ensuring that plants receive optimal conditions for trichome development. Additionally, hydroponic and aeroponic systems offer faster nutrient uptake, potentially leading to increased resin production compared to traditional soil cultivation.

Supplemental methods, such as organic amendments, beneficial microorganisms, or specific additives, are incorporated to enhance resin production. Organic supplements, such as guano or bat droppings, are rich in phosphorus and potassium, promoting robust trichome development. Beneficial microorganisms, including mycorrhizae and certain bacteria, form symbiotic relationships with the plant roots, enhancing nutrient absorption and overall plant health. Specialized additives, such as bloom boosters or resin enhancers, are designed to provide additional support during the flowering stage.

Post-harvest practices, such as proper drying and curing, are essential to preserving and maximizing the resin content of buds. Slow and controlled drying processes, conducted in a dark, well-ventilated space with optimal humidity levels, help maintain the integrity of cannabinoids and terpenes. Curing involves storing dried buds in airtight containers, allowing them to undergo a slow and controlled fermentation process. This enhances the development of flavors, aromas, and the overall quality of the resinous end product.

In conclusion, maximizing resin production for potent buds requires a multifaceted approach that combines genetic selection, environmental optimization, and targeted cultivation practices. Growers can enhance trichome development and resin synthesis by choosing high-resin strains, creating an optimal growing environment, adjusting nutrient regimens, implementing strategic pruning and training, and applying stress-inducing techniques. Advanced cultivation methods, supplemental additives, and thoughtful post-harvest practices further contribute to the overall goal of producing cannabis with elevated potency and quality. With a holistic approach that encompasses the entire cultivation process, growers can unlock the full potential of resin production, resulting in potent, high-quality buds sought after by cannabis enthusiasts and medicinal users alike.

CHAPTER VIII

Harvesting Your Crop

Determining the right time to harvest

Determining the right time to harvest is a crucial decision that significantly influences the final crop's potency, flavor, and overall quality. Harvesting cannabis at the peak of its maturity ensures the maximum concentration of cannabinoids, terpenes, and other valuable compounds. Deciding when to harvest involves carefully observing the plant's physiological changes, particularly in developing trichomes – the tiny, resinous glands that house cannabinoids and terpenes. As cannabis plants progress through the flowering stage, trichomes undergo distinct transformations, and these changes serve as critical indicators for growers aiming to pinpoint the optimal harvest window.

One of the primary indicators of a plant's readiness for harvest is the appearance of trichomes on the flowers. Trichomes transition through different stages during the flowering period, evolving from clear to cloudy and, in some cases, developing amber hues. Clear trichomes are typically observed early in the flowering stage, indicating a lower concentration of cannabinoids and suggesting that the plant is not yet at its peak potency. As the flowering phase progresses, trichomes become cloudy or milky, signaling the accumulation of cannabinoids like THC and CBD. This stage is often considered the peak of cannabinoid production, contributing to the euphoric and therapeutic effects associated with cannabis consumption. Growers aiming for a well-balanced blend of cannabinoids and a euphoric high often choose to harvest during this cloudy trichome stage.

In addition to cloudy trichomes, some cultivators look for the appearance of amber-colored trichomes as an additional indicator of readiness. Amber trichomes suggest further breaking down cannabinoids, mainly THC, into degraded forms. Harvesting during this stage may result in a more soothing or relaxing effect, making it a preferred choice for those seeking cannabis with potential medicinal benefits for conditions such as insomnia or anxiety. The cloudy to amber trichomes ratio becomes a critical consideration for growers tailoring their harvest to achieve specific effects.

Magnification tools, such as a jeweler's loupe or a microscope, are commonplace for growers seeking precision in determining trichome maturity. Close examination of trichomes under magnification allows growers to observe the subtle color changes and assess the ratio of clear, cloudy, and amber trichomes. This level of scrutiny enables growers to make informed decisions based on the specific characteristics they desire in the final product. It's important to note that trichome development can vary between cannabis strains, emphasizing the need for strain-specific observations.

Beyond trichome appearance, other visual cues on the plant can assist in determining the right time to harvest. Observing the color and state of the pistils – the hair-like structures on the flowers – provides additional insights. During the early stages of flowering, pistils are often white and vibrant. As the plant matures, these pistils change color, with many turning amber or brown. While pistil color change can indicate general maturity, it is not as precise as trichome observation and is often used as a secondary visual cue.

The harvest timing also depends on the desired effect and the cultivated strain. Sativa-dominant strains may be harvested later in the window of trichome development to achieve a more energetic and uplifting effect. Indica-dominant strains, on the other hand, might be harvested slightly earlier, emphasizing the cloudy trichome stage, to preserve a more relaxing and soothing profile. Hybrid strains, which combine Indica and sativa characteristics, allow for a nuanced approach to harvesting, catering to the desired effects the cultivator seeks.

Environmental factors, such as the plant's exposure to light, can impact the timing of trichome development and influence the harvest decision. Cannabis plants exposed to intense sunlight, especially ultraviolet (UV) light, often produce more trichomes as a protective response. Therefore, growers using supplemental UV light during the flowering stage may observe an increase in trichome density, potentially affecting the overall potency of the harvest. Adjusting light conditions and ensuring consistency during the flowering phase contribute to predictable trichome development and facilitate accurate timing for harvest.

The maturation of the plant's flowers is not uniform, and different parts of the same plant may reach optimal maturity at other times. As a result, some growers choose a phased or selective harvesting approach, allowing them to harvest individual branches or buds as they reach their peak. This method caters to the variability in trichome development across the plant, ensuring that each harvested portion is maximally potent. While this approach requires more attention and effort, it gives growers more significant control over the final composition and effects of the harvested cannabis.

Cannabis plants are known for their ability to exhibit distinct growth patterns and responses based on genetics, environmental conditions, and cultivation practices.

Therefore, the right time to harvest can also be influenced by the specific goals of the grower. Some cultivators may opt for an early harvest to capture a more cerebral or clear-headed high. In contrast, others may choose a later harvest for a more soothing or relaxing experience. The variability in harvest timing allows growers to customize their approach based on their preferences and the desired effects for the end users.

The method of harvest, whether performed manually or mechanically, is another consideration in the cultivation process. Hand harvesting allows for a more selective approach, with experienced growers targeting individual buds or branches. This method ensures precision in harvesting at the desired trichome stage. Mechanical harvesting, on the other hand, is more efficient but may result in a less selective harvest, potentially including buds at different stages of maturity. The choice between manual and mechanical harvesting depends on the scale of cultivation, available resources, and the desired level of control over the harvest process.

Post-harvest handling is a critical phase in maintaining the quality of the harvested cannabis. Proper drying and curing procedures are essential to preserve the buds' potency, flavor, and aroma. Slow and controlled drying in a dark, well-ventilated space prevents the degradation of cannabinoids and terpenes. Curing involves storing dried buds in airtight containers, allowing them to undergo a slow fermentation process that enhances the development of flavors and aromas. The commitment to thorough post-harvest practices ensures the carefully timed harvest results in a premium and well-preserved end product.

In conclusion, determining the right time to harvest cannabis is a nuanced and multifaceted process that requires a keen understanding of the plant's life cycle, genetic characteristics, and environmental influences.

The visual observation of trichome development, supported by magnification tools, is a primary indicator of maturity. Additional cues, such as pistil color change and overall plant development, contribute to the decision-making process. The timing of harvest is a pivotal factor in shaping the final product's potency, effects, and overall quality. With careful consideration of these factors, growers can master the art of harvesting cannabis at its peak, delivering a potent and premium experience for consumers.

Techniques for harvesting, trimming, and curing

The techniques for harvesting, trimming, and curing cannabis are crucial components of the post-flowering process that significantly impact the quality, potency, and overall experience of the final product. As cannabis reaches its peak maturity during the flowering stage, the careful execution of these techniques ensures that the delicate trichomes, containing cannabinoids and terpenes, are preserved and maximized. Harvesting marks the commencement of this process, requiring precise timing and attention to detail. Once harvested, the buds undergo trimming to remove excess foliage and prepare them for consumption. Subsequently, curing becomes a critical step, involving a gradual drying and fermentation process that refines the flavors, aromas, and potency of the cannabis. Each of these stages requires a nuanced approach to maintain the integrity of the plant and deliver a premium product to consumers.

Harvesting is a pivotal moment in the cannabis cultivation process, marking the culmination of weeks of careful monitoring and anticipation. The ideal time to harvest is determined by the visual cues provided by the trichomes, the small resinous glands that house cannabinoids and terpenes. As trichomes transition from clear to cloudy or amber, growers harvest at the peak of cannabinoid production, flavor development, and potency. The use of magnification tools, such as a jeweler's loupe or a microscope, aids in precise trichome observation. Once the optimal trichome maturity is identified, the plant is carefully harvested, either manually or mechanically, to preserve the delicate structures and prevent unnecessary damage to the buds.

Trimming follows the harvest, serving as a meticulous process to refine the appearance and composition of the buds. The primary goal of trimming is to remove excess leaves, stems, and other non-cannabinoid-bearing plant material, enhancing the buds' visual appeal and overall quality. Hand trimming allows for a more selective approach, with experienced trimmers targeting individual buds to preserve trichomes and maintain the desired appearance. Alternatively, mechanical trimming may be employed for efficiency, though it runs the risk of being less precise and potentially causing more significant disruption to trichome integrity. Effective trimming is essential for creating a visually appealing and market-ready product regardless of the chosen method.

Curing is the final and perhaps most underrated stage in the post-harvest process, yet it plays a pivotal role in refining the flavors, aromas, and overall quality of the cannabis buds. Curing involves gradual drying and fermentation of the harvested buds in a controlled environment. Proper curing not only preserves the potency of cannabinoids but also allows for the development of complex terpene profiles, contributing to the nuanced flavors and aromas associated with high-quality cannabis. The process typically occurs in airtight containers, which are periodically opened to release moisture and promote airflow. Depending on the desired outcome, this controlled drying and fermentation process can last several weeks to months.

During the initial curing phase, excess moisture is gradually released from the buds, reducing the risk of mold and ensuring a smooth smoking experience. Simultaneously, the slow oxidation of cannabinoids and terpenes takes place, enhancing their chemical composition and contributing to the evolution of flavor and aroma. Curing also allows for the breakdown of chlorophyll, the green pigment in plants, which can impart a harsh taste if not adequately addressed. As chlorophyll breaks down, the final product becomes smoother and more palatable.

Proper curing conditions are crucial for achieving the desired results. The ideal curing environment maintains a relative humidity (RH) level between 55% and 62%, preventing the buds from becoming too dry or retaining excessive moisture. Temperature control is equally important, with most cultivators opting for a dark, excellent space to slow down the curing process and preserve the delicate compounds within the buds. Adequate ventilation, achieved by periodically opening the curing containers, prevents excess moisture buildup and encourages the continuation of the curing process.

The choice of curing containers also plays a role in the overall success of the process. Glass jars with airtight seals are popular choices, as they provide an impenetrable environment that allows for controlled curing. While aesthetically pleasing, wooden containers may impart unwanted flavors to the buds. The size of the curing containers should be appropriate for the quantity of cannabis being cured, as larger containers may hinder proper moisture release and airflow.

While many growers prioritize curing for its impact on flavor and aroma, it also has implications for the overall potency of the cannabis. The slow degradation of tetrahydrocannabinolic acid (THCA) into delta-9-tetrahydrocannabinol (THC) occurs during curing, potentially increasing the psychoactive effects of the final product. This conversion is influenced by temperature, humidity, and light exposure, emphasizing the importance of maintaining optimal curing conditions to achieve the desired balance of cannabinoids and terpenes.

Beyond flavor and potency, the curing process also affects the texture and appearance of the buds. Well-cured cannabis typically exhibits a desirable level of moisture content, resulting in a balanced and pliable texture. Overly dry cannabis may crumble and lack the resinous stickiness associated with fresh, well-cured buds. Properly cured buds also maintain their vibrant colors and trichome coverage, contributing to an appealing visual presentation.

The duration of curing varies based on individual preferences and desired outcomes. Some cultivators opt for a shorter cure of a few weeks, prioritizing the preservation of fresher flavors and a more pronounced "green" aroma. Others prefer an extended treatment, allowing for a more profound development of terpene profiles and a smoother overall smoking experience. The strain, environmental conditions, and the desired characteristics of the final product often influence the decision on curing duration.

Regular monitoring and assessment of the buds are essential throughout the curing process. This involves inspecting the texture, aroma, and moisture content to ensure optimal curing conditions. Overly moist buds may develop mold, while excessively dry buds may lose their terpene richness. Adjustments can be made by introducing or limiting airflow, changing the size of curing containers, or modifying environmental conditions to maintain the desired RH level.

In conclusion, the techniques for harvesting, trimming, and curing cannabis are integral to the post-flowering process, shaping the final quality, potency, and overall experience of the product. Harvesting at the peak of trichome maturity, careful trimming to enhance visual appeal and methodical curing to refine flavors and aromas collectively contribute to a premium cannabis product. The art of curing, often overlooked, is a transformative stage that harmonizes cannabinoids and terpenes, producing a well-rounded and enjoyable end product. By mastering these techniques, cultivators can deliver a consistently exceptional cannabis experience to consumers, showcasing the full potential of the plant and the craftsmanship involved in its cultivation.

Preservation and storage tips for long-lasting quality

Preserving and storing cannabis properly is paramount for maintaining its long-lasting quality, potency, and overall integrity. Whether cultivated for personal use or acquired from a legal dispensary, cannabis enthusiasts and patients alike can benefit from understanding the best practices for storage. Exposure to light, air, heat, and moisture can all contribute to the degradation of cannabinoids, terpenes, and other valuable compounds present in the plant. To ensure that the characteristics of the cannabis remain intact over time, it is essential to adopt practical preservation and storage strategies.

One of the primary considerations in cannabis storage is protecting the buds from exposure to light. Light, especially ultraviolet (UV) light, can degrade cannabinoids and terpenes, compromising the overall quality of the product. As such, it is advisable to store cannabis in opaque containers that block out light. Dark glass jars or metal containers are famous for preserving the plant material. Additionally, keeping cannabis in a dark and relaxed environment, away from direct sunlight, further minimizes the risk of light-induced degradation.

Air is another factor that can impact the long-term quality of cannabis. Oxygen, in particular, can lead to the oxidation of cannabinoids and the breakdown of terpenes. To mitigate this, storage containers should be airtight to minimize exposure to the surrounding air. Vacuum-sealed containers or jars with tight-fitting lids help create an oxygen-free environment, preserving the freshness and potency of the buds. It is worth noting that excessive handling and unnecessary opening of storage containers can introduce air and compromise the intended storage conditions.

Temperature control is a critical aspect of cannabis preservation. Cannabis is best stored in a relaxed and stable environment to slow down the degradation process. Excessive heat can accelerate the breakdown of cannabinoids and terpenes, potentially diminishing the therapeutic and psychoactive effects of the product. Ideally, cannabis should be stored in a place where temperatures remain consistent, avoiding fluctuations that could impact its overall quality. Refrigeration is often discouraged due to the risk of introducing moisture when containers are taken in and out of cold storage.

Moisture content in stored cannabis is a crucial consideration. Too much moisture can create an environment conducive to mold and mildew growth, while overly dry conditions can result in brittle and harsh-tasting buds. Relative humidity (RH) levels between 55% and 62% are generally recommended for optimal cannabis storage. Humidity packs or control devices specifically designed for cannabis storage can help maintain the ideal moisture balance. It is advisable to check the RH levels periodically and replace humidity packs to ensure consistent conditions.

Choosing the correct storage container is integral to practical preservation. Glass jars with airtight seals are commonly preferred to maintain freshness without imparting unwanted flavors to the cannabis. Dark-colored glass jars offer the added benefit of blocking out light. Some cannabis enthusiasts opt for specialty storage containers equipped with built-in humidity control mechanisms, providing an all-in-one solution for preserving the plant material.

In addition to container selection, the way cannabis is packaged within those containers matters. Buds should be stored in a manner that minimizes unnecessary compression or agitation. Using containers that closely match the quantity of cannabis being stored helps prevent excessive air exposure when opening and closing the container. For larger quantities, dividing the cannabis into smaller portions reduces the frequency of opening the storage container, contributing to long-term preservation.

Labeling containers with pertinent information, such as the strain name, harvest date, and any other relevant details, can be beneficial for both personal and legal compliance reasons. This information not only allows users to track the age and origin of the cannabis but also provides a means of distinguishing between different strains and their unique characteristics. Proper labeling enhances organization and facilitates a more informed and enjoyable cannabis experience.

For those looking to store cannabis for an extended period, freezing is an option to consider. Freezing can slow down the degradation process by reducing the activity of enzymes and slowing down chemical reactions. However, freezing cannabis requires meticulous preparation to minimize potential moisture issues. Buds should be thoroughly dried before freezing to prevent the formation of ice crystals, which can damage the delicate trichomes. Additionally, cannabis should be sealed in airtight, moisture-resistant packaging before being placed in the freezer. When removing cannabis from the freezer, allowing it to come to room temperature before opening the container is crucial to prevent condensation.

It's important to note that freezing may not be suitable for all types of cannabis products. The texture and consistency of certain products, such as concentrates or infused edibles, may be altered by freezing. Therefore, the decision to freeze cannabis should be based on the specific product and its intended use.

In conclusion, adopting proper preservation and storage practices is essential for maintaining the long-lasting quality of cannabis. Protecting the plant material from light, air, heat, and moisture helps preserve cannabinoids, terpenes, and freshness. Choosing the correct storage container, maintaining appropriate humidity levels, and avoiding unnecessary exposure to the surrounding environment contribute to the longevity of cannabis quality. Whether stored for personal enjoyment or medicinal use, implementing these strategies ensures that cannabis enthusiasts can consistently experience the full spectrum of effects and flavors that the plant has to offer. By treating cannabis with care and attention throughout its storage journey, users can maximize their enjoyment of this versatile and cherished botanical product.

CHAPTER IX

Troubleshooting Common Issues

Identifying and addressing common problems

Identifying and addressing common problems in cannabis cultivation is essential to ensuring a successful and bountiful harvest. Cultivators encounter various challenges throughout the plant's lifecycle, from germination to flowering, and understanding how to recognize and effectively address these issues is critical to maintaining a healthy crop. One prevalent challenge is pests, which can manifest in various forms, including spider mites, aphids, and caterpillars. Early detection is crucial, and cultivators should regularly inspect their plants for signs of infestation, such as discolored or damaged leaves, webs, or visible pests. Natural predators, like ladybugs or predatory mites, can be introduced as a biological control method, while insecticidal soaps and neem oil offer non-toxic options for pest management.

Another common issue is nutrient deficiencies or imbalances, often evidenced by yellowing or discolored leaves, stunted growth, or abnormal leaf patterns. Soil or nutrient testing can help identify weaknesses, allowing growers to adjust their fertilization practices accordingly. It's important to note that over-fertilization can be as detrimental as under-fertilization, so maintaining a balanced nutrient regimen is crucial. Changing pH levels, providing a well-rounded fertilizer, and incorporating organic amendments can help address nutrient-related challenges and promote healthy plant development.

Environmental factors like temperature and humidity fluctuations can pose significant challenges. High temperatures can lead to heat stress, causing wilting, leaf curling, or even bud damage. Adequate ventilation, shading, and cooling methods like fans or air conditioning can help mitigate heat-related issues. Conversely, low temperatures can slow growth and impact nutrient absorption. Protective measures like adding insulation, using heat mats, or employing greenhouse structures can provide a controlled environment for optimal growth. Maintaining the proper humidity levels, typically lower during flowering to prevent mold, is essential, and dehumidifiers or adequate ventilation systems can assist in regulating humidity.

Watering practices also play a crucial role in preventing issues such as root rot or nutrient leaching. Overwatering can lead to waterlogged soil, depriving the roots of oxygen and promoting the growth of harmful pathogens. On the other hand, underwatering can result in nutrient deficiencies and hinder overall plant development. Implementing a consistent watering schedule, monitoring soil moisture levels, and ensuring proper drainage are effective strategies to address water-related challenges.

Pathogens and diseases, including powdery mildew, mold, or bacterial infections, pose a constant threat to cannabis crops. Prevention is critical, and cultivators can implement measures such as proper spacing between plants to improve airflow, maintaining cleanliness in the growing environment, and using disease-resistant strains. Fungicides, bio-fungicides, or natural remedies like neem oil can be employed to address pathogen-related challenges. Regularly inspecting plants for any signs of disease and promptly isolating or treating affected plants can help prevent the spread of pathogens throughout the crop.

Improper pH levels in the growing medium can result in nutrient uptake issues, impacting plant health and development. Cannabis plants generally thrive in slightly acidic to neutral pH ranges. Regularly testing and adjusting the pH of the soil or hydroponic solution is crucial for preventing nutrient lockout and ensuring optimal nutrient absorption. pH imbalances can be corrected using pH-adjusting solutions or amendments, bringing the growing medium back to the desired range.

Cannabis cultivators may also encounter challenges related to plant structure and growth. Issues such as stretching, where plants grow tall and spindly, can be attributed to inadequate light intensity or incorrect light spectrum during the vegetative stage. Adjusting lighting conditions or optimizing the light source can help address stretching problems. Conversely, stunted growth may result from insufficient nutrients, poor soil quality, or environmental stressors. Identifying the underlying cause and implementing corrective measures, such as adjusting nutrient levels or improving soil conditions, is crucial for fostering healthy plant growth.

During the flowering stage, hermaphroditism, or the development of both male and female reproductive organs, can be a significant concern. Hermaphroditic plants can lead to unwanted pollination and seed development, diminishing the harvest quality. Regularly inspecting plants for the presence of male flowers and promptly removing them can help prevent the risk of pollination. Stress management, maintaining stable environmental conditions, and using feminized seeds can also contribute to minimizing the occurrence of hermaphroditism.

Addressing these common problems requires a combination of vigilance, proactive management, and a solid understanding of the cannabis plant's requirements at each stage of its life cycle. Cultivators should be prepared to adjust their cultivation practices based on their plants' specific needs and challenges. Regular monitoring, timely interventions, and a holistic approach to plant care contribute to a successful cultivation experience, yielding a robust and high-quality cannabis harvest. As the cannabis industry continues to evolve, cultivators are encouraged to stay informed about advancements in cultivation techniques, pest management strategies, and disease prevention to optimize their growing practices and maximize the potential of their cannabis crops.

Tips for preventing pests, diseases, and nutrient deficiencies

Maintaining a healthy and thriving cannabis garden requires diligent efforts to prevent pests, diseases, and nutrient deficiencies that can compromise the overall well-being of the plants. A proactive cultivation approach is essential, starting with a robust pest prevention strategy. Regularly monitoring plants for signs of pests, such as spider mites, aphids, or caterpillars, is crucial for early detection. Introducing beneficial insects, such as ladybugs or predatory mites, is a natural and sustainable method for controlling pest populations. Additionally, preventive measures like neem oil or insecticidal soaps can deter common cannabis pests without resorting to harsh chemicals.

Disease prevention is equally vital in cannabis cultivation. Creating an environment that minimizes the risk of pathogens, such as powdery mildew or mold, is fundamental. Adequate spacing between plants to promote airflow, maintaining optimal humidity levels, and regularly cleaning and disinfecting cultivation equipment help mitigate the risk of diseases spreading. Choosing disease-resistant strains, implementing proper ventilation systems, and ensuring a clean and sanitized grow space contribute to a proactive defense against potential pathogens.

Nutrient deficiencies or imbalances can significantly impact plant health and development. Cultivators should prioritize soil or nutrient testing to assess the composition of the growing medium and adjust nutrient regimens accordingly. Striking the right balance is essential, as both under-fertilization and over-fertilization can lead to adverse effects. Monitoring pH levels is another critical aspect of nutrient management, as deviations from the optimal pH range can result in nutrient lockout. Regular adjustments using pH-balancing solutions or amendments help maintain the proper nutrient uptake by the plants, fostering healthy growth.

Preventive strategies for pests, diseases, and nutrient deficiencies extend to environmental management. Controlling temperature and humidity levels is crucial, as fluctuations can create conditions favorable to pests and diseases. High temperatures may lead to heat stress and increased pest activity, while excessive humidity can contribute to mold growth. Maintaining a stable and controlled environment through proper ventilation, shading, and climate control systems is integral to preventing these issues. Investing in quality lighting systems tailored to the specific needs of cannabis plants contributes to vigorous growth and helps prevent stretching or other light-related problems.

The selection of disease-resistant cannabis strains is a proactive measure that aligns with an overall prevention strategy. By choosing genetics with inherent resistance to common pests and diseases, cultivators can reduce the likelihood of encountering these issues during the cultivation process. Disease-resistant strains are often bred to withstand specific environmental stressors, making them well-suited for outdoor or greenhouse cultivation, where exposure to pests and diseases may be more challenging to control.

An essential component of preventing nutrient deficiencies is adopting a comprehensive fertilization plan that addresses the specific needs of cannabis plants at different growth stages. Understanding the nutrient requirements during the vegetative and flowering phases allows cultivators to tailor their feeding schedules accordingly. Regular soil testing or nutrient analysis of hydroponic solutions provides valuable insights into the nutrient composition and aids in making informed adjustments to the fertilization regimen. Organic amendments, such as compost or well-aged manure, can be incorporated into the soil to enhance its nutrient content and microbial activity, promoting a healthy and well-balanced growing medium.

Implementing good cultivation practices is an overarching strategy for preventing many issues in cannabis cultivation. This includes maintaining proper hygiene in the grow space by regularly cleaning equipment, removing debris, and disinfecting surfaces. Sterilizing tools between uses helps prevent the spread of pests and diseases. Proper sanitation extends to personal hygiene practices, with growers taking precautions to avoid introducing contaminants into the cultivation area. This includes washing hands and changing clothing before entering the grow space to minimize the risk of cross-contamination.

Furthermore, crop rotation, or changing the location of cannabis plants within a grow space, can be an effective preventive measure. This disrupts the life cycle of potential pests and diseases specific to certain plants. Additionally, rotating crops in outdoor cultivation minimizes the depletion of particular nutrients in the soil, promoting a more sustainable and balanced ecosystem.

Mulching is a practice that conserves moisture, regulates soil temperature, and contributes to pest prevention. Organic mulches, such as straw or wood chips, create a barrier that deters certain pests from reaching the soil and the base of the plants. Mulching also promotes soil health by fostering microbial activity and improving overall structure.

Education and ongoing learning are essential aspects of preventing and addressing challenges in cannabis cultivation. Staying informed about the latest advancements in pest management, disease prevention, and nutrient optimization allows cultivators to adapt their practices based on industry best practices and emerging research. Networking with other cultivators, participating in community forums, and attending industry events provide valuable opportunities to exchange knowledge and learn from shared experiences.

In conclusion, preventing pests, diseases, and nutrient deficiencies in cannabis cultivation requires a multifaceted and proactive approach. From adopting integrated pest management strategies to selecting disease-resistant strains, maintaining optimal environmental conditions, and implementing comprehensive fertilization plans, cultivators play a crucial role in fostering a resilient and healthy cannabis garden. By incorporating preventive measures into their cultivation practices, growers can minimize the risk of issues that could compromise the quality and yield of their cannabis crop. Through continuous education, adaptation, and a commitment to best practices, cultivators can navigate the challenges of cannabis cultivation successfully and contribute to the sustainability of this dynamic and evolving industry.

Troubleshooting guide for overall plant health

A comprehensive troubleshooting guide for overall plant health is indispensable for cannabis cultivators seeking to identify and address various issues that may arise during the plant's life cycle. One of the common challenges is nutrient deficiencies, which can manifest through symptoms such as yellowing leaves, stunted growth, or abnormal discoloration. Cultivators must closely examine these symptoms and consider factors such as pH levels, nutrient concentrations, and soil quality to pinpoint the underlying cause. Adjusting nutrient regimens, incorporating organic amendments, and maintaining optimal pH levels are vital interventions to address nutrient-related challenges and restore plant health.

Pests pose a persistent threat to cannabis cultivation, and early detection is crucial for effective management. Spider mites, aphids, and caterpillars are common culprits that can damage plants. Visual inspection, especially under leaves and at the growing tips, helps identify the presence of pests. Integrated pest management (IPM) practices, including introducing natural predators, using neem oil or insecticidal soaps, and maintaining a clean and sanitized grow space, are essential components of a robust strategy to combat pest infestations and protect overall plant health.

Diseases like powdery mildew, mold, or bacterial infections can harm plant health and productivity. Early recognition of disease symptoms, including unusual spotting, discoloration, or visible signs of mold, is crucial. Cultivators should implement preventive measures, including proper spacing between plants, ventilation systems, and the use of disease-resistant strains. In cases where diseases are identified, prompt intervention with fungicides, bio fungicides, or natural remedies is necessary to prevent the spread and mitigate the impact on overall plant health.

Environmental factors play a significant role in overall plant health, and fluctuations in temperature and humidity can lead to stress and adverse effects on growth. Heat stress, characterized by wilting, leaf curling, or bud damage, can occur in high-temperature conditions. Adequate ventilation, shading, and cooling methods are essential to address heat-related challenges. Conversely, low temperatures can slow growth and impede nutrient absorption, necessitating insulation, heating mats, or greenhouse structures to provide a conducive environment for optimal plant development. Maintaining stable environmental conditions and appropriate humidity levels contributes to plant resilience and health.

Watering practices are critical considerations in troubleshooting plant health. Overwatering can result in waterlogged soil, leading to root rot and nutrient deficiencies, while underwatering can stunt growth and impede nutrient uptake. Cultivators should adopt a consistent watering schedule, monitor soil moisture levels, and ensure proper drainage to prevent water-related challenges. Additionally, water quality for irrigation is essential, as water with high mineral content or contaminants can adversely affect plant health. Regular testing and treatment of irrigation water contribute to a proactive approach to maintaining overall plant health.

Structural issues like stretching or stunted growth may arise from inadequate lighting conditions. Pulling, characterized by tall and spindly growth, indicates insufficient light intensity during vegetative. Adjusting lighting conditions or optimizing the light source can address stretching problems. Conversely, stunted growth may result from nutrient deficiencies, poor soil quality, or environmental stressors. Identifying the cause and implementing corrective measures, such as adjusting nutrient levels or improving soil conditions, is crucial for promoting healthy plant growth and overall vigor.

Cultivators must also be vigilant for signs of hermaphroditism, where plants develop both male and female reproductive organs. This phenomenon poses a risk of unwanted pollination and seed development, negatively impacting the harvest quality. Regular inspection for male flowers and prompt removal, along with stress management and the use of feminized seeds, can help minimize the occurrence of hermaphroditism and maintain overall plant health.

Addressing challenges in overall plant health requires a holistic understanding of the cannabis plant's life cycle, environmental requirements, and potential stressors. The troubleshooting guide encompasses a range of factors, from nutrient management and pest control to ecological conditions and structural considerations. Cultivators are encouraged to adopt an integrated and systematic approach, regularly monitoring plants and proactively identifying and addressing issues as they arise. Continuous learning, adaptability, and adherence to best practices contribute to the overall success of cannabis cultivation and the promotion of robust and healthy plants from seedling to harvest.

CHAPTER X

Advanced Growing Techniques

Exploring advanced cultivation methods

Exploring advanced cultivation methods represents a dynamic frontier in the ever-evolving world of cannabis cultivation, where innovative techniques and cutting-edge technologies are pushing the boundaries of what is achievable regarding plant health, yield optimization, and quality enhancement. One of the noteworthy advancements in cultivation is the integration of precision agriculture, leveraging data-driven approaches and sensor technologies to monitor and optimize various environmental factors. This allows cultivators to fine-tune temperature, humidity, and light intensity variables, creating an ideal and highly controlled growth environment. Automated systems, equipped with sensors and artificial intelligence, enable real-time adjustments to cultivation parameters, ensuring optimal conditions for plant growth throughout the entire life cycle.

Hydroponics and Aeroponics are advanced cultivation methods that have gained popularity for their ability to provide a precisely controlled nutrient delivery system to plants. Hydroponic systems utilize a soilless medium, such as perlite or coco coir, and a nutrient-rich solution to deliver essential elements directly to the plant roots. Conversely, Aeroponics suspends plant roots in a nutrient-rich mist, promoting efficient nutrient absorption. These methods enhance nutrient uptake, accelerate growth rates, and allow for more precise control over the plant's nutritional profile. Hydroponic and aeroponic systems can be tailored to recirculate and conserve water, contributing to sustainable cultivation practices.

Light-emitting diode (LED) technology has revolutionized how cultivators approach indoor cultivation lighting. LED grow lights offer customizable spectra tailored to different stages of plant growth, providing an energy-efficient and cost-effective alternative to traditional high-intensity discharge (HID) lights. The ability to fine-tune light spectra allows cultivators to optimize photosynthetic efficiency and influence plant morphology, resulting in improved yields and enhanced cannabinoid and terpene profiles. Furthermore, LED lights produce less heat, reducing the need for additional climate control measures and contributing to a more environmentally sustainable cultivation process.

Vertical farming represents a space-efficient and innovative cultivation method that has gained traction in urban environments where space is limited. Cultivators can maximize available space by stacking growing layers vertically, effectively increasing the cultivation footprint. Vertical farming systems often incorporate advanced automation, climate control, and hydroponic or aeroponic technologies to create a controlled and efficient cultivation environment. This approach allows for higher yields in smaller spaces and reduces the environmental impact associated with traditional horizontal farming practices.

Regenerative agriculture is an advanced cultivation approach that strongly emphasizes soil health, biodiversity, and sustainability. This method prioritizes organic and regenerative practices to enhance soil fertility, reduce environmental impact, and promote overall ecosystem health. Techniques such as cover cropping, crop rotation, and composting are integral to regenerative agriculture, fostering a holistic and balanced ecosystem within the cultivation environment. By prioritizing soil health, regenerative agriculture contributes to the long-term sustainability of cannabis cultivation while producing high-quality, organically- grown cannabis.

Cannabis tissue culture is emerging as a groundbreaking method for cloning and propagating plants in a controlled and sterile environment. Tissue culture involves taking small tissue samples from the mother plant and culturing them in a nutrient-rich medium under hygienic conditions. This method eliminates the risk of pathogens and diseases, ensuring the production of genetically identical and disease-free plants. Tissue culture allows for preserving and propagating elite genetics, streamlining the cloning process, and contributing to consistent and high-quality plant production.

Utilizing beneficial microbes and mycorrhizal fungi represents an advanced cultivation method that enhances soil health and nutrient absorption. These microorganisms form symbiotic relationships with plant roots, aiding nutrient cycling, pathogen resistance, and overall plant vigor. Incorporating microbial inoculants into the cultivation process fosters a living soil ecosystem, contributing to improved plant resilience, enhanced terpene production, and increased nutrient availability. This approach aligns with sustainable cultivation practices, reducing the reliance on synthetic fertilizers and promoting a more balanced and natural ecosystem within the soil.

Blockchain technology is making inroads into the cannabis industry, offering solutions to transparency, traceability, and compliance challenges. Through blockchain-based systems, cultivators can track the entire lifecycle of a cannabis plant, from seed to sale. This level of transparency ensures compliance with regulatory standards and provides consumers with verifiable information about the origin, cultivation practices, and testing results of the cannabis products they purchase. By leveraging blockchain technology, cultivators can instill greater confidence in consumers and regulatory bodies, fostering accountability and transparency in the cannabis supply chain.

Incorporating machine learning and artificial intelligence (AI) into cultivation practices represents a paradigm shift in optimizing plant growth and resource efficiency. AI systems can analyze vast amounts of data related to environmental conditions, plant health, and cultivation practices, providing insights and recommendations for optimal decision-making. This technology enables cultivators to identify patterns, predict potential issues, and adjust cultivation parameters in real time. By harnessing the power of AI, cultivators can achieve higher yields, reduce resource waste, and enhance overall efficiency in cannabis cultivation.

In conclusion, exploring advanced cultivation methods in the cannabis industry is paving the way for innovative and sustainable approaches to plant cultivation. From precision agriculture and hydroponics to LED lighting, vertical farming, regenerative agriculture, tissue culture, microbial inoculants, blockchain technology, and artificial intelligence, cultivators now have diverse tools and techniques at their disposal. These advancements not only contribute to increased yields and improved product quality but also address critical challenges related to environmental impact, resource efficiency, and compliance. As the cannabis industry continues to evolve, embracing and implementing these advanced cultivation methods will play a pivotal role in shaping the future of sustainable and high-tech cannabis cultivation practices.

Hydroponics, Aeroponics, and other cutting-edge approaches

Hydroponics, Aeroponics, and other cutting-edge cultivation approaches represent a transformative shift in how cannabis is grown, leveraging advanced techniques to maximize efficiency, optimize nutrient delivery, and enhance overall plant health. Hydroponics, a soilless cultivation method, delivers nutrient-rich solutions directly to the plant roots. This method eliminates the need for traditional soil, allowing cultivators precise control over the nutrient composition and uptake. Hydroponic systems range from simple nutrient film techniques (NFT) to more complex deep water culture (DWC) systems. These systems accelerate growth rates, reduce water consumption, and enable cultivators to tailor nutrient formulations, producing robust plants with enhanced cannabinoid and terpene profiles.

Aeroponics takes precision cultivation further by suspending plant roots in a nutrient-rich mist, promoting efficient nutrient absorption. This method offers a highly oxygenated environment for the roots, facilitating rapid nutrient uptake and plant growth. Aeroponic systems excel in delivering nutrients directly to the root zone, minimizing waste, and optimizing resource utilization. The increased oxygen exposure to the roots also enhances plant health, contributing to faster growth, increased yields, and improved nutrient efficiency. Both hydroponics and Aeroponics exemplify how innovative cultivation methods can revolutionize traditional approaches, providing cultivators unprecedented control and efficiency.

Vertical farming represents a space-efficient and technologically advanced approach to cannabis cultivation. In vertical farming systems, plants are stacked in multiple layers, maximizing available space and significantly increasing the cultivation capacity. This method is precious in urban environments where space is limited. Vertical farms often integrate hydroponic or aeroponic systems, automated climate control, and LED lighting to create a controlled and efficient growing environment. Vertical stacking and advanced technologies allow cultivators to achieve higher yields while conserving resources and reducing the environmental footprint associated with traditional horizontal farming.

The integration of light-emitting diode (LED) technology has revolutionized indoor cannabis cultivation by providing energy-efficient, customizable, and spectrum-tailored lighting solutions. LED grow lights emit light in specific spectra that align with plants' photosynthetic needs at different growth stages. Unlike traditional high-intensity discharge (HID) lights, LEDs produce less heat, reducing the need for additional climate control measures. Cultivators can fine-tune light spectra to influence plant morphology, optimize photosynthetic efficiency, and enhance the production of cannabinoids and terpenes. LED technology contributes to energy savings and allows for more precise control over the growing environment, leading to healthier plants and improved overall cultivation outcomes.

Regenerative agriculture is gaining prominence as a cutting-edge and sustainable cultivation approach, strongly emphasizing soil health, biodiversity, and ecosystem balance. This method prioritizes organic and regenerative practices such as cover cropping, crop rotation, and composting to enhance soil fertility and reduce the environmental impact of cultivation. By fostering a holistic and balanced ecosystem within the soil, regenerative agriculture promotes resilience to pests and diseases, increases water retention, and ultimately contributes to the long-term sustainability of cannabis cultivation. The regenerative approach aligns with the growing demand for environmentally conscious and ethically produced cannabis products.

Tissue culture is an innovative method that has revolutionized plant propagation by providing a sterile and controlled environment for cloning. Tissue culture involves taking small tissue samples from the mother plant and cultivating them in a nutrient-rich medium under hygienic conditions. This eliminates the risk of pathogens and diseases, ensuring the production of genetically identical and disease-free plants. Tissue culture offers a reliable and efficient means of preserving elite genetics, streamlining the cloning process, and contributing to consistent and high-quality plant production. This approach exemplifies how advanced techniques can revolutionize traditional propagation methods, offering increased precision and reliability.

Integrating beneficial microbes and mycorrhizal fungi into cultivation practices is another cutting-edge approach to enhancing soil health and nutrient absorption. These microorganisms form symbiotic relationships with plant roots, promoting nutrient cycling, improving pathogen resistance, and enhancing plant vigor. Cultivators can foster a living soil ecosystem by incorporating microbial inoculants into the cultivation process, contributing to improved plant resilience, enhanced terpene production, and increased nutrient availability. This approach aligns with sustainable cultivation practices, reducing the reliance on synthetic fertilizers and promoting a more balanced and natural ecosystem within the soil.

Blockchain technology is making strides in the cannabis industry, offering solutions to transparency, traceability, and compliance challenges. Blockchain-based systems enable cultivators to track the entire lifecycle of a cannabis plant, from seed to sale. This level of transparency ensures compliance with regulatory standards and provides consumers with verifiable information about the origin, cultivation practices, and testing results of the cannabis products they purchase. By leveraging blockchain technology, cultivators can instill greater confidence in consumers and regulatory bodies, fostering accountability and transparency in the cannabis supply chain.

Artificial intelligence (AI) and machine learning technologies are increasingly finding applications in cannabis cultivation, providing insights and recommendations for optimal decision-making. AI systems analyze vast amounts of data related to environmental conditions, plant health, and cultivation practices, allowing cultivators to identify patterns, predict potential issues, and dynamically adjust cultivation parameters in real time. By harnessing the power of AI, cultivators can achieve higher yields, reduce resource waste, and enhance overall efficiency in cannabis cultivation. These technologies exemplify how the convergence of data analytics and cultivation practices can lead to more informed and responsive approaches to plant management.

In conclusion, hydroponics, Aeroponics, and other cutting-edge cultivation approaches represent a paradigm shift in the cannabis industry, offering innovative solutions to traditional cultivation challenges. These methods showcase the industry's commitment to sustainability, precision, and efficiency, with technologies such as LED lighting, vertical farming, regenerative agriculture, tissue culture, microbial inoculants, blockchain, and AI playing pivotal roles in shaping the future of cannabis cultivation. As the industry continues to evolve, cultivators embracing these advanced techniques are poised to increase yields and product quality and contribute to a more sustainable and technologically sophisticated cannabis cultivation landscape.

Fine-tuning your skills for exceptional yields

Fine-tuning cultivation skills is an ongoing and essential process for cannabis cultivators aspiring to achieve exceptional yields and consistently high-quality harvests. Mastery of the cultivation craft involves a deep understanding of the cannabis plant's biology, its environmental requirements, and the ability to adapt and optimize cultivation practices throughout its life cycle. The journey begins with selecting premium genetics, as the foundation of a successful harvest lies in the quality of the plant material. Choosing strains that align with cultivation goals, whether focused on high cannabinoid content, specific terpene profiles, or resilience to environmental stressors, sets the stage for a successful cultivation endeavor.

Accurate environmental control is paramount in fine-tuning cultivation skills. Cultivators must meticulously manage variables such as temperature, humidity, and light intensity to create an optimal growing environment. Maintaining balance fosters vigorous plant growth, maximizes photosynthetic efficiency, and minimizes stressors hindering yields. Utilizing climate control systems, ventilation, and shading techniques allows cultivators to create a stable and controlled environment, ensuring the cannabis plants thrive throughout the vegetative and flowering stages.

Nutrient management is a crucial aspect of skillful cultivation, demanding a nuanced understanding of the cannabis plant's nutritional needs at different growth stages. Fine-tuning nutrient solutions involves regular monitoring of soil or hydroponic solution composition, adjusting formulations based on plant responses, and ensuring the right balance of essential elements. Cultivators often incorporate organic amendments, such as compost or well-aged manure, to enhance soil structure and microbial activity. The ability to interpret nutrient deficiencies or excesses and make precise adjustments contributes to the overall health and vitality of the plants, ultimately influencing yield and product quality.

Precision in irrigation practices is a hallmark of skilled cultivation. Overwatering or underwatering can lead to various issues, including root rot, nutrient deficiencies, or stunted growth. Fine-tuning irrigation involves a consistent watering schedule, monitoring soil moisture levels, and ensuring proper drainage. The water quality used for irrigation is equally critical, as water with high mineral content or contaminants can impact plant health. Cultivators who master the art of irrigation contribute to optimal root health, nutrient uptake, and overall plant resilience.

Training and pruning techniques are integral to fine-tuning cultivation skills to achieve exceptional yields. Strategic pruning and training influence the plant's structure, maximizing light exposure to lower bud sites and promoting an even canopy. Techniques such as topping, low-stress training (LST), and defoliation require careful consideration of the plant's growth patterns and responses. Skilled cultivators understand how to manipulate the plant's architecture to optimize bud development, increase airflow, and manage overall plant health. These practices contribute to uniform bud development and improved light penetration, producing higher yields of premium-quality flowers.

Monitoring and managing pests and diseases require a keen eye and a proactive approach. Skilled cultivators regularly inspect plants for signs of infestations or infections, employing integrated pest management (IPM) strategies to mitigate risks. This may include introducing beneficial insects, applying natural remedies like neem oil, or implementing cultural practices that discourage pest proliferation. Identifying potential issues early and implementing targeted interventions contribute to plant health, minimizing the impact of pests and diseases on yields and product quality.

Fine-tuning cultivation skills extend into the flowering stage, where optimizing light cycles plays a pivotal role. Cultivators manipulating fair schedules can induce flowering, manage stretch during the transition, and maximize resin production. Understanding the specific light requirements during the flowering stage allows precise control over the plant's physiological responses, resulting in denser and more potent buds. Skilled cultivators may employ techniques such as extending the dark period, utilizing supplemental lighting, or incorporating light movers to ensure uniform, fair distribution, contributing to exceptional yields of high-quality cannabis flowers.

Harvest timing is a critical skill that distinguishes experienced cultivators. Determining the right time to harvest involves monitoring trichome development, observing changes in bud structure, and assessing overall plant health. Cultivators must balance maximizing cannabinoid and terpene content and avoiding degradation or overripening. Fine-tuning the harvesting process, including proper trimming and curing techniques, contributes to preserving cannabinoids and terpenes, resulting in a final product with enhanced potency, flavor, and overall appeal.

Continual education and adaptability are inherent to fine-tuning cultivation skills. Staying informed about advancements in cultivation techniques, pest management strategies, and industry trends ensures cultivators remain at the forefront of their craft. Engaging with the cannabis cultivation community, attending industry events, and seeking out relevant publications contribute to ongoing learning and skill refinement. Cultivators who embrace a continuous improvement mindset are better equipped to navigate challenges, incorporate new technologies, and consistently achieve exceptional yields.

In conclusion, fine-tuning cultivation skills is an intricate and evolving process requiring knowledge, experience, and adaptability. From selecting premium genetics to mastering environmental control, nutrient management, irrigation practices, and advanced cultivation techniques, skilled cultivators navigate the complexities of the cannabis plant's life cycle with precision. Pursuing exceptional yields involves a commitment to continuous learning, adaptability, and understanding the interconnected factors influencing plant health and productivity. Cultivators who hone their skills contribute to their success and the advancement of sustainable and high-quality cannabis cultivation practices.

CHAPTER XI

The Legal Landscape of Cannabis

Overview of marijuana laws and regulations

The landscape of marijuana laws and regulations is complex and continually evolving, reflecting the shifting attitudes towards cannabis worldwide. While some regions have embraced legalization for medical or recreational use, others maintain strict prohibitions. Understanding this intricate tapestry requires examining the diverse approaches adopted by various jurisdictions. In countries like Canada and Uruguay, cannabis has been fully legalized for recreational use, allowing adults to purchase, possess, and consume cannabis within specified limits. In the United States, the situation is nuanced, with several states legalizing cannabis for both medical and recreational purposes while others maintain strict prohibitions. This patchwork of state-level regulations coexists with federal prohibition, creating legal and regulatory challenges for businesses and consumers.

Medical marijuana legalization has gained traction in numerous jurisdictions, recognizing cannabis's therapeutic potential and providing patients with access to cannabis-based medications. In these cases, individuals with qualifying medical conditions can obtain medical cannabis recommendations from healthcare professionals, allowing them to access cannabis products through licensed dispensaries. The medical marijuana framework often includes regulations governing the cultivation, distribution, and sale of medical cannabis, as well as patient registration and identification systems.

Regulations surrounding the cultivation and distribution of cannabis vary widely, with some jurisdictions allowing for private cultivation and others maintaining a tightly controlled, licensed system. Licensed cannabis producers must adhere to stringent quality and safety standards, undergo rigorous testing procedures, and comply with regulatory requirements to ensure consumer safety. Distribution channels, whether through government-run stores, licensed dispensaries, or a combination of both, are subject to specific regulations governing licensing, product labeling, advertising, and age restrictions.

Beyond recreational and medical use, industrial hemp has become a focal point in many jurisdictions, driven by its versatility and economic potential. Hemp contains minimal THC, the psychoactive compound found in cannabis, and is primarily cultivated for its fibers, seeds, and oil. Many countries have legalized the cultivation of industrial hemp, paving the way for a range of industries, including textiles, food products, and biofuels. Regulations surrounding hemp cultivation often involve licensing, testing for THC content, and adherence to agricultural practices.

The international landscape of cannabis laws further complicates the regulatory framework with significant approach variations. Some countries have adopted a liberal stance, while others strictly enforce prohibition. The United Nations Single Convention on Narcotic Drugs of 1961 remains a cornerstone international treaty addressing the control and regulation of cannabis and other narcotics. However, shifts in attitudes towards cannabis have prompted discussions and reconsideration of global drug policy.

Social equity and justice have become central considerations in the ongoing dialogue about cannabis laws and regulations. Historically, cannabis prohibition disproportionately affected marginalized communities, leading to disparities in arrest and incarceration rates. As jurisdictions move towards legalization, there is a growing recognition of the need to address these historical injustices. Some regions have incorporated social equity provisions into their cannabis regulations, aiming to redress the impact of the war on drugs by promoting inclusivity, diversity, and opportunities for those disproportionately affected.

Public opinion plays a significant role in shaping marijuana laws and regulations, and as societal attitudes evolve, so do the legal frameworks governing cannabis. Scientific research continues to contribute to the understanding of cannabis's medicinal properties, therapeutic potential, and potential risks. This evolving knowledge base informs policymakers as they craft regulations that balance public health and safety considerations with individual freedoms and economic opportunities.

While the trend toward cannabis legalization and decriminalization is evident in various parts of the world, challenges persist. Regulatory frameworks must strike a delicate balance, addressing public health concerns, preventing illicit activities, and fostering a responsible cannabis industry. Issues such as impaired driving, youth access, and the potential for addiction necessitate robust regulations and comprehensive public education campaigns.

In conclusion, the overview of marijuana laws and regulations reveals a diverse and dynamic landscape shaped by cultural, social, economic, and scientific factors. From full legalization for recreational use to strict prohibition, each jurisdiction adopts an approach that reflects its unique considerations and priorities. As the global conversation surrounding cannabis continues to evolve, the need for comprehensive and adaptable regulatory frameworks becomes increasingly apparent. Striking the right balance between individual liberties, public health, and social equity remains a complex challenge, and the ongoing evolution of marijuana laws reflects a collective effort to navigate this intricate terrain.

Navigating legal challenges for home cultivation

Navigating legal challenges for home cultivation of cannabis involves carefully examining the laws and regulations specific to the jurisdiction in which one resides. While the landscape surrounding cannabis is evolving, marked by increasing acceptance and legalization in various regions, the permissibility of home cultivation can vary significantly. In jurisdictions where cannabis is fully legalized, either for medical or recreational purposes, individuals may enjoy the right to cultivate a limited number of plants for personal use. However, even in such cases, specific regulations regarding the number of plants, cultivation methods, and storage often apply, and individuals must familiarize themselves with these guidelines to avoid unintentional legal violations.

In regions where cannabis remains prohibited or only legalized for medical use, home cultivation may be strictly forbidden. Violating these restrictions can result in legal consequences, ranging from fines to criminal charges. Therefore, individuals must exercise caution and awareness of local laws before attempting to cultivate cannabis at home. The legal status of cannabis is subject to change, driven by shifting societal attitudes, scientific research, and legislative initiatives. Staying informed about the latest legal developments ensures that individuals are aware of any alterations to home cultivation regulations and can adapt their practices accordingly.

Medical marijuana laws often include provisions allowing patients to cultivate cannabis plants for personal use. However, there are usually strict guidelines and limitations even in these cases. Patients must typically register with relevant authorities, obtain a medical cannabis recommendation from a qualified healthcare professional, and adhere to specific cultivation limits. Understanding the nuances of medical marijuana laws is crucial to ensuring compliance and avoiding legal repercussions. Additionally, some jurisdictions that have legalized recreational cannabis may offer specific allowances for medical patients, allowing them to cultivate more plants or possess a higher quantity of cannabis.

Beyond the number of plants permitted, legal challenges for home cultivation may also involve restrictions on cultivation methods. For instance, certain jurisdictions may only allow indoor cultivation to minimize the risk of diversion to the illicit market or prevent the cultivation from being visible to the public. Compliance with these regulations may require individuals to invest in indoor growing equipment, such as grow tents, lighting systems, and ventilation, adding a layer of complexity to home cultivation.

Privacy concerns are another legal aspect to consider when cultivating cannabis at home. Some jurisdictions mandate that cultivation activities be conducted discreetly, out of public view. This may involve implementing security measures to protect the privacy of the cultivation space and prevent unauthorized access. Home cultivators must also be mindful of odor control to avoid potential nuisance complaints from neighbors, which could result in legal consequences.

Zoning regulations may further impact the legal landscape of home cultivation. Local ordinances and zoning laws can dictate where cannabis cultivation is permitted, potentially restricting it to certain areas or types of residences. Individuals must research and understand these zoning regulations to ensure compliance with local laws. Failure to adhere to zoning restrictions can lead to legal consequences, including fines or orders to cease cultivation activities.

The legality of sharing or gifting homegrown cannabis is an additional legal consideration for home cultivators. While cultivating cannabis for personal use may be permitted in certain jurisdictions, transmitting or distributing cannabis without the appropriate licenses may still be illegal. Understanding the regulations around sharing homegrown cannabis is essential to avoid legal complications.

In some regions, legal challenges for home cultivation may extend to issues related to child protection. Cannabis cultivation spaces must be secure and inaccessible to minors to comply with child safety regulations. Failure to implement adequate security measures may result in legal consequences, particularly if children can access cannabis plants or related paraphernalia.

Compliance with environmental regulations is another facet of navigating legal challenges for home cultivation. Some jurisdictions may restrict water usage, electrical consumption, fertilizers, and pesticides. Home cultivators must know and adhere to these regulations to avoid environmental violations and associated legal consequences.

Community standards and homeowner association rules can also impact the legal landscape of home cultivation. In areas governed by homeowners' associations (HOAs), specific rules may prohibit cannabis cultivation, even if permitted at the state or municipal level. Understanding and respecting these community standards is vital to maintaining a harmonious living environment and avoiding potential legal disputes with the HOA.

Navigating legal challenges for home cultivation requires a comprehensive understanding of the laws and regulations applicable to one's location. Individuals must keep abreast of changes in cannabis laws, zoning regulations, and local ordinances to ensure compliance. Seeking legal advice or consultation with experts in cannabis law can provide valuable insights and guidance, helping individuals navigate the intricate legal landscape of home cultivation responsibly and within the bounds of the law. As the cannabis regulatory framework evolves, staying informed and adaptable remains paramount for those engaging in home cultivation practices.

Staying informed and compliant with local regulations

Staying informed and compliant with local regulations is paramount for individuals engaging in any aspect of the cannabis industry, including cultivation, distribution, or consumption. The legal landscape surrounding cannabis is dynamic and can vary significantly from one jurisdiction to another. Whether driven by medical, recreational, or industrial considerations, cannabis regulations are subject to frequent changes and updates. Therefore, individuals must remain vigilant, continuously educate themselves about the latest developments, and adapt their practices to avoid legal complications.

For those involved in cannabis cultivation, whether at a commercial scale or for personal use, a fundamental step in staying compliant is understanding and adhering to local laws. This involves thorough research into municipal, state, and national regulations governing cannabis cultivation activities. Different regions may have distinct guidelines regarding the number of plants permitted, cultivation methods allowed, and security measures required. Compliance with these regulations is crucial not only to prevent legal consequences but also to contribute to the overall legitimacy and sustainability of the cannabis industry.

Local zoning regulations play a crucial role in determining where cannabis-related activities are permitted. Municipalities often have zoning ordinances that dictate where cultivation facilities, dispensaries, and other cannabis-related businesses can operate. Understanding these zoning regulations is essential for prospective business owners to select appropriate locations for their operations and avoid potential legal challenges. Zoning laws may also impact home cultivation, dictating whether cannabis cultivation is allowed in residential areas and specifying any additional requirements for those engaged in personal cultivation.

Staying informed about changes in cannabis laws requires continuous monitoring of legislative developments at various levels of government. This involves keeping abreast of proposed bills, amendments, and regulatory updates that could impact the cannabis industry. Engaging with advocacy groups, industry associations, and legal experts can provide valuable insights and timely information about impending changes to cannabis regulations. Proactively seeking relevant information helps individuals and businesses stay ahead of regulatory shifts and make informed decisions about their involvement in the cannabis space.

Collaborating with legal professionals who specialize in cannabis law is an integral aspect of staying compliant with local regulations. Cannabis laws can be intricate, and legal advice from professionals familiar with the specific nuances of the industry is invaluable. Attorneys specializing in cannabis law can guide licensing requirements, zoning considerations, health and safety regulations compliance, and other legal aspects unique to the cannabis sector. Establishing a relationship with legal counsel ensures that individuals and businesses have a trusted resource for advice and assistance in navigating the complexities of cannabis regulations.

Comprehensive compliance programs are essential for businesses operating in the cannabis industry. This involves developing internal policies and procedures that align with local regulations and industry best practices. Compliance programs should cover areas such as inventory tracking, security protocols, employee training, record-keeping, and adherence to quality and safety standards. Implementing robust compliance measures ensures adherence to local regulations and fosters a culture of responsibility and legitimacy within the cannabis business.

Education and training are critical components of staying compliant in the dynamic cannabis industry. For businesses, this involves educating employees about local regulations, company policies, and best practices. Regular training sessions help reinforce compliance expectations and inform staff about regulation changes. For individuals engaged in personal cultivation, staying educated about local laws and best cultivation practices is essential. This may involve attending workshops and seminars or accessing online resources that provide up-to-date information on cannabis regulations and cultivation techniques.

Engaging with the local community and building positive relationships can improve compliance and acceptance. Transparent communication with neighbors, local authorities, and community members can address concerns, dispel misconceptions, and foster a supportive environment for cannabis-related activities. Community engagement also provides an opportunity to showcase responsible and compliant practices, contributing to a positive perception of the cannabis industry within the broader community.

Regular monitoring and auditing of operations are critical for businesses and individuals to ensure compliance with local regulations. This involves conducting internal assessments to identify any areas of potential non-compliance and taking corrective action promptly. Businesses may also undergo external audits or inspections by regulatory authorities, emphasizing the importance of maintaining meticulous records and demonstrating a commitment to regulations.

In conclusion, staying informed and compliant with local regulations is an ongoing commitment for individuals and businesses involved in the cannabis industry. Whether cultivating cannabis, operating a dispensary, or engaging in related activities, a thorough understanding of the legal landscape is essential. This involves continuous education, collaboration with legal professionals, development of comprehensive compliance programs, engagement with the local community, and a proactive approach to monitoring and auditing operations. By prioritizing compliance, individuals and businesses contribute to the sustainability and legitimacy of the cannabis industry, fostering an environment that aligns with evolving regulations and societal expectations.

CHAPTER XII

Cultivating Responsibly

Sustainable and eco-friendly growing practices

Embracing sustainable and eco-friendly growing practices is a fundamental aspect of responsible cannabis cultivation that aligns with the broader movement towards environmental stewardship. As the cannabis industry continues to expand, there is a growing recognition of the environmental impact associated with cultivation practices. Sustainable growing aims to mitigate these impacts by adopting practices prioritizing environmental health, resource conservation, and ecological balance.

Water conservation is a central pillar of sustainable growing practices. Traditional cultivation methods, especially in outdoor settings, can be water-intensive. Sustainable approaches include implementing efficient irrigation systems, harvesting rainwater, and using drought-resistant cannabis strains. Additionally, the recycling and reclamation of water runoff can reduce water consumption. By prioritizing water conservation, cultivators not only address environmental concerns but also enhance the resilience of their operations in the face of changing climatic conditions and water scarcity challenges.

Energy efficiency is another critical component of sustainable cultivation. Indoor cultivation facilities often require substantial energy inputs for lighting, ventilation, and climate control. Sustainable practices in this context involve using energy-efficient technologies, such as LED lighting, which reduces energy consumption and minimizes heat output, alleviating the need for additional cooling systems. Integrating renewable energy sources, such as solar or wind power, further enhances the sustainability of indoor cultivation operations. By prioritizing energy efficiency, cultivators can significantly reduce their carbon footprint and contribute to the overall environmental goals of the industry.

Soil health and conservation are integral aspects of sustainable growing practices. Traditional agricultural practices, including some cannabis cultivation methods, can lead to soil degradation, loss of biodiversity, and erosion. Sustainable cultivation involves adopting regenerative agriculture techniques such as cover cropping, crop rotation, and organic soil amendments. These practices enhance soil structure, promote microbial diversity, and improve nutrient retention, contributing to long-term soil health. Additionally, avoiding synthetic pesticides and fertilizers helps prevent soil contamination and promotes a balanced and thriving ecosystem within the soil.

The responsible use of nutrients is crucial for sustainable cannabis cultivation. Excessive use of synthetic fertilizers can lead to nutrient runoff, negatively impacting water sources and aquatic ecosystems. Sustainable practices emphasize precision in nutrient management, utilizing organic fertilizers, compost, and other natural amendments to provide the necessary nutrients for plant growth. Implementing nutrient cycling techniques, such as composting plant waste, contributes to a closed-loop system that minimizes external inputs and reduces environmental impact.

Biodiversity conservation is a crucial principle of sustainable growing practices. Monoculture, or the cultivation of a single crop over large areas, can lead to imbalances in ecosystems and increased vulnerability to pests and diseases. Sustainable cultivation involves creating diverse and resilient ecosystems that support a variety of plant and animal species. Integrating companion planting, where beneficial plants are strategically placed to enhance pest control or nutrient availability, is one way to promote biodiversity. Additionally, preserving natural habitats and minimizing harmful pesticides contribute to the overall ecological balance surrounding cultivation sites.

Waste reduction and responsible disposal practices are essential components of sustainable cannabis cultivation. The industry generates various forms of waste, including plant trimmings, packaging materials, and non-recyclable items. Sustainable approaches involve recycling, composting, and reusing waste materials wherever possible. Composting plant waste reduces the environmental impact and creates nutrient-rich compost that can be reintegrated into the cultivation process. Minimizing single-use plastics and adopting eco-friendly packaging options further contribute to waste reduction efforts.

Sustainable and eco-friendly practices extend beyond cultivation techniques to encompass the entire supply chain, including packaging, transportation, and distribution. Sustainable packaging choices, such as biodegradable or recyclable materials, contribute to reducing the environmental footprint of cannabis products. Implementing energy-efficient transportation methods and distribution practices further aligns with sustainability goals. Cultivators and industry stakeholders committed to holistic sustainability prioritize environmentally conscious choices at every stage of the cannabis production and distribution process.

Certification programs and industry standards have emerged to recognize and promote sustainable cultivation practices. Certifications, such as the Clean Green Certified program, focus on verifying organic and sustainable cultivation methods within the cannabis industry. By adhering to these standards, cultivators signal their commitment to environmental responsibility and provide consumers with a means to make informed choices about environmentally friendly products. These certification programs contribute to building a sustainable and ethical cannabis industry that prioritizes ecological health and consumer well-being.

Education and advocacy are vital in promoting sustainable growing practices within the cannabis industry. Cultivators benefit from staying informed about the latest advancements in sustainable technologies, cultivation techniques, and environmental best practices. Industry events, workshops, and collaborative platforms provide opportunities for knowledge exchange and collective efforts towards sustainability. By fostering a culture of sustainability within the cannabis community, stakeholders can collectively address environmental challenges and work towards a more ecologically conscious future for the industry.

In conclusion, sustainable and eco-friendly growing practices are essential for the responsible and ethical development of the cannabis industry. By prioritizing water conservation, energy efficiency, soil health, biodiversity, waste reduction, and environmentally conscious supply chain practices, cultivators contribute to the overall sustainability of cannabis cultivation. As the industry continues to evolve, embracing and championing these sustainable practices is a commitment to environmental stewardship and a response to the growing demand for ethically produced and ecologically responsible cannabis products. Cultivating a sustainable future for the cannabis industry involves a collective effort to balance economic goals with environmental responsibility, ultimately shaping an industry that thrives in harmony with the natural world.

Ethical considerations in the marijuana industry

Ethical considerations in the marijuana industry are increasingly recognized as essential components of responsible and sustainable business practices. As the cannabis sector evolves, stakeholders grapple with complex ethical dilemmas that span cultivation, distribution, marketing, and consumption. Central to these considerations is the need to balance economic interests with moral responsibilities, ensuring that the industry's growth aligns with social justice, equity, and environmental sustainability principles.

One critical ethical consideration revolves around social equity and justice within the marijuana industry. Historically, cannabis prohibition disproportionately affected marginalized communities, resulting in high arrest and incarceration rates. As legalization efforts gain traction, there is a growing acknowledgment of the need to address and rectify these historical injustices. Ethical operators in the industry actively seek ways to promote inclusivity, diversity, and opportunities for individuals whom the war has disproportionately impacted on drugs. This may involve implementing social equity programs, supporting minority-owned businesses, and advocating for policies prioritizing restorative justice measures for affected communities.

Environmental sustainability is another critical ethical consideration in the marijuana industry. As cannabis cultivation expands, concerns arise about the ecological impact of large-scale operations, particularly those employing resource-intensive practices. Virtuous cultivators recognize the importance of adopting sustainable growing methods, such as organic farming, water conservation, and energy-efficient technologies. Initiatives like regenerative agriculture, which focuses on restoring and improving soil health, exemplify ethical commitments to minimizing ecological footprints and preserving natural resources.

Responsible marketing practices are integral to ethical considerations in the marijuana industry. Given the complex history of cannabis and its association with counterculture, there is a need for ethical marketing that avoids reinforcing stereotypes or targeting vulnerable populations. Ethical marketing extends to promoting accurate information about cannabis products, preventing misleading claims, and adhering to regulations governing the promotion of cannabis. Cultivators and distributors committed to ethical marketing prioritize consumer education, transparency, and responsible advertising to foster a positive and informed cannabis culture.

Labor practices within the marijuana industry are a focal point of ethical considerations. As the industry expands, ensuring fair wages, safe working conditions, and employee rights becomes paramount. Honest employers prioritize creating a workplace culture that values diversity, equity, and inclusion. This involves implementing anti-discrimination policies, offering training programs, and providing opportunities for professional development. Ethical considerations extend beyond the immediate workforce to encompass the entire supply chain, promoting fair and honest practices among suppliers and partners.

Community engagement is a crucial ethical consideration for businesses operating in the marijuana industry. Establishing positive relationships with local communities involves transparent communication, addressing concerns, and contributing to the community's overall well-being. Ethical operators engage in initiatives that benefit local economies, support community organizations, and foster a positive perception of the cannabis industry. By actively participating in community dialogue and addressing the specific needs of the areas where they operate, ethical businesses contribute to the social fabric and acceptance of cannabis within society.

Ensuring product safety and quality is an ethical imperative within the marijuana industry. Virtuous cultivators and manufacturers prioritize rigorous testing procedures to guarantee that cannabis products meet quality standards and are contaminants-free. This commitment to product safety extends to accurate labeling, providing consumers with transparent information about cannabinoid content, potential allergens, and cultivation methods. Ethical considerations in product safety also involve clear instructions for responsible consumption, particularly in the case of edibles and other infused products.

Ethical considerations extend to responsible consumption practices and promoting a culture of moderation. While cannabis has therapeutic and recreational potential, honest operators in the industry recognize the importance of encouraging responsible use. This involves educating consumers about dosage, potential risks, and the importance of avoiding impaired activities such as driving under the influence. Ethical retailers may implement measures to prevent sales to minors and actively engage in public education campaigns to promote a balanced and informed approach to cannabis consumption.

Ethical considerations also encompass intellectual property rights, fair competition, and preventing the exploitation of indigenous knowledge. As the cannabis industry evolves, issues related to patents, trademarks, and proprietary strains may arise. Ethical operators prioritize respecting the intellectual property of others, avoiding unfair competition practices, and recognizing the value of indigenous cannabis knowledge. Collaborative efforts that acknowledge and include the perspectives of diverse communities contribute to a more equitable and ethical industry landscape.

Transparency and accountability are overarching ethical principles that guide responsible conduct within the marijuana industry. Honest operators prioritize open communication with stakeholders, including consumers, employees, regulatory authorities, and the wider community. Transparent business practices involve disclosing information about cultivation methods, sourcing, testing protocols, and potential conflicts of interest. Accountability includes acknowledging mistakes, rectifying errors, and actively participating in efforts to address industry challenges collaboratively. Ethical businesses operate with integrity, demonstrating a commitment to ethical considerations beyond compliance with regulations.

In conclusion, ethical considerations in the marijuana industry are vital for shaping a responsible and sustainable future for the sector. From social equity and environmental sustainability to responsible marketing, labor practices, and community engagement, ethical operators prioritize values that extend beyond mere profitability. As the industry matures, integrating ethical considerations becomes not only a business imperative but also a moral obligation. By fostering a culture of responsibility, inclusion, and transparency, the marijuana industry can contribute to positive social change, challenge historical injustices, and create a foundation for a resilient and ethically sound future.

CONCLUSION

In conclusion, "Green Thumb Chronicles: The Art of Growing Exceptional Weed - From Seed to Harvest, Mastering the Marijuana Garden" is an invaluable guide for novice and experienced cannabis cultivators. This comprehensive and meticulously crafted book navigates the reader through every stage of the cultivation process, offering a wealth of knowledge, insights, and practical tips. From germinating seeds to navigating the complexities of flowering and harvesting, the book delves into the intricacies of cannabis cultivation with clarity and expertise.

One of the book's standout features is its emphasis on responsible and sustainable cultivation practices. The author provides detailed instructions for achieving optimal yields and underscores the importance of ethical considerations, environmental sustainability, and compliance with local regulations. Including sections on social equity, ethical marketing, and community engagement demonstrates a commitment to fostering a positive and inclusive cannabis culture.

The author's dedication to education is evident throughout the book, emphasizing continuous learning and staying informed about the latest developments in the cannabis industry. This commitment reflects the dynamic nature of cannabis cultivation, where evolving technologies, legal landscapes, and community expectations necessitate cultivators to be adaptable and well-informed.

Moreover, "Green Thumb Chronicles" goes beyond the technical aspects of cultivation, addressing broader topics such as the historical context of cannabis prohibition, the significance of social equity, and the ethical responsibilities of cultivators. This holistic approach sets the book apart, providing readers with a well-rounded understanding of the cannabis industry and their role within it.

Overall, "Green Thumb Chronicles" is not just a guide; it is a companion for those embarking on the journey of cannabis cultivation. It encourages a responsible, informed, and ethical approach, fostering a community of cultivators who are proficient in the art of growing exceptional weed and stewards of an industry that values inclusivity, sustainability, and responsible practices. Whether cultivating for personal use or considering a commercial venture, readers of this book are equipped with the knowledge and mindset needed to navigate the complexities of the marijuana garden with skill and responsibility.

Thank you for buying and reading/listening to our book. If you found this book useful/helpful please take a few minutes and leave a review on the platform where you purchased our book. Your feedback matters greatly to us.

www.ingramcontent.com/pod-product-compliance
Lightning Source LLC
Chambersburg PA
CBHW052040150726
48002CB00002B/685